RAGTIME
REDISCOVERIES

RAGTIME REDISCOVERIES

64 Works from the Golden Age of Rag

Selected and with an Introduction by

Trebor Jay Tichenor

Dover Publications, Inc., New York

PUBLISHER'S NOTE

Since the originals reproduced here are faithful historical documents as well as sources of enjoyment, the titles, textual material and artwork have not been changed even where they reflect the broader humor of their era, in which the nation was far less sensitive to jibes about minority groups. It is our belief that a mature understanding of our past is more fruitful than a falsification of history.

ACKNOWLEDGMENTS

Much of the following ragtime lore is gratefully borrowed from *They All Played Ragtime* by Rudi Blesh and Harriet Janis (Quick-Fox, Inc., New York), the ragtimers' "bible."

Such an in-depth compilation of rags as the present volume is possible only through the enthusiastic cooperation of fellow collectors and historians. A complete list of all ragtime friends and musicians is always impossible, but I would like to thank the following for lending rare originals and furnishing valuable information: Mike Montgomery, Thornton Hagert, Dave Jasen, Harold and Thelma Doerr, Alice and Dewey Green, Elliott Adams, Ed Spankle, Tex Wyndham and The Ragtime Society of Canada, Dick Zimmerman of the Maple Leaf Club, Bob Wright, Bob Ault, Eric Sager, Albert Mothershead of the St. Louis Ragtime Guild, Mike Schwimmer, Al Rose, Bob Darch, Roger C. Hankins, William Russell, Frank Powers, Mrs. Olav Ekrom, Sam Clark, Richard B. Allen, Ben Conroy, Bly Corning, Joseph R. Scotti, and my own St. Louis Ragtimers.

Ragtime Rediscoveries: 64 Works from the Golden Age of Rag is a new collection of music, selected and with an introduction by Trebor Jay Tichenor, first published by Dover Publications, Inc., in 1979. The original publishers and dates of publication of the music appear in the Contents and on the individual covers and title pages.

International Standard Book Number: 0-486-23776-1
Library of Congress Catalog Card Number: 78-73573

Manufactured in the United States of America
Dover Publications, Inc.
180 Varick Street
New York, N.Y. 10014

INTRODUCTION

The 1890's were a time of musical revolution in America: a new sound called ragtime burst upon the scene, displacing the maudlin sentimentality, the pallid importations of the Victorian era—syncopation now ruled the nation. Ragtime had a freshness, a power and conception that belied a rather haphazard development out of a complex nineteenth-century musical ferment. And the threads may never be completely unraveled—the phonograph came too late for us to hear how it happened. But there is no doubt that the rag has Afro-American folk roots; while the true sounds of older black music are forever lost—the juba dances, plantation fiddles and banjos—the spirit is reflected in the popular music of the blackface minstrels of that day. The seeds of our native music were sown here in such tunes as "Old Dan Tucker" and "Zip Coon," as imported music traditions became enriched with an amalgam of folk elements, both black and white.

The hallmark of this transformation was a restless energy, a brash optimism that was expressed through syncopation. At some point lost to memory the idea of a consistently syncopated melodic line played against a regular-metered march bass was tried out on the piano. The place of origin was the "underground"—the saloons and pleasure emporiums of the late nineteenth century where itinerant black pianists transformed the old marches, quadrilles and schottisches into syncopation. Keyboard instruments had been generally inaccessible to black people before the Civil War, and were much sought after later. Many of the pioneers, including Eubie Blake, began by ragging familiar tunes on the family reed organ—usually inspiring parental ire. Ragtime thus began as a way of playing—a style of creative, syncopated transformation and embellishment of a melody. In the early days it was called "jig piano," referring back to the old minstrel dances, and favorite targets were old standards such as "Annie Laurie."

Capturing these folk ragtime ideas on paper was an art that evolved in the late '90's—most of the earliest scored syncopations were piano arrangements of popular songs done by schooled arrangers of the larger publishing houses.

The character of the rag was evolving: at first, a random collection of syncopated themes—medleys of idiomatic pop tunes such as the "coon songs," and occasionally genuine folk melodies—by 1897 the whole concept had matured; rags appeared which were organized collections of *original* syncopated themes. Ragtime was becoming a through-composed art, a piano literature. As the rag evolved, much form and flavor were derived from the march and the old-world dances. A rag is usually a construction of three to four separate strains; each one is played and then repeated (sometimes with embellishments), and the tune moves on to the next one. This concept is non-developmental in the classical sense, and unlike jazz, which evolves from improvisation on a theme. Within this discipline ragtime composers continued to find new ways to express themselves. The sound of a rag may vary from the formality of a Missouri classic to the bouncing rhythm of a fox-trot. It was a new music, a purely American concoction of formal and folk traditions. It expressed the imagination and dynamism of turn-of-the century America, when the country was young and adventuresome in spirit.

America was ready for the rag; the parlor piano was a fixture, a status symbol in American homes then, and more people made their own music, either by hand or by foot-pumping the pedals of the new pianola. Ragtime became our musical language for over two decades; it transformed our dancing, beginning with the cakewalk and evolving through the turkey trot of the 'teens.

But the rag did not arrive without a fight. A Coxey's Army of vociferous critics objected strenuously to the new ragged syncopations; taken as a group they were almost totally uninformed. In the early years they fussed and fumed that ragtime was the work of Satan—sinful and degenerate music of low-life origins. At least one tried to prove that merely hearing a rag could induce a spontaneous, involuntary reaction akin to an epileptic fit ("Ragtime: the New Tarantism"). Later on these bilious Brahmins confused the rags with the popular songs of the day and never mentioned Scott Joplin; it was a sign of what happened to the genuine article. Ragtime became a craze, a highly profitable business.

The popular song has always been the main staple of the music business, and, as Tin Pan Alley moved closer to centralizing the entire publishing output of the country, America was flooded with syncopated songs and simple rags. At least by 1910 everything that was syncopated was called a rag. Much fine syncopated playing was widespread in arrangements and renditions of popular songs, especially on piano rolls—a continuation of the old tradition of creative performance and transformation. But the genuine rag was a separate, more complex instrumental conception, a more abstract form in the tradition of absolute music. The rags are the *crème de la crème*, one of our richest musical legacies.

The '70's have seen an unparalleled revival of ragtime, and a new academic interest in the form. America now thinks of ragtime more in terms of a graceful Scott Joplin rag than a fast, triple-forte rendition of an old pop song banged out on an out-of-tune upright piano. This is indeed a joyful progress for the genuine rag! Scott Joplin has at last intoxicated America with his beautiful, bittersweet classic rags.

The Missouri legacy of Scott Joplin and his peers is a rich one, to be sure, but not our total legacy of ragtime; it is high time to widen our scope, to appreciate all the other gifted men and women composers who syncopated with a flair. The present revival has centered on Joplin, barely allowing a glance at other composers. This single focus has thrown the rest of ragtime far *out* of focus. It has fostered a completely mistaken notion not only at the popular level, but also at the academic, that the classic Missouri school was the musical clearing house for all ragtime activity that preceded it, and the source, the inspiration for everything else that followed. The pioneer classic rag publisher, John Stark, helped perpetuate this myth in his hyperbolic ads which insisted that the Stark rags were the "simon pure," and that everything else was a "pale imitation." The label "classic rag" was an appropriate choice to proclaim the rags of Joplin, Scott, Lamb, et al., as truly immortal works. But the classic rag form was also just one way of organizing folk materials and writing ragtime. From 1897 on there were publishers all over the country who, like Stark, published ragtime they believed in. Composers and performers everywhere were producing excellent ragtime, and much of it was more syncopated, more "raggy" than the formal classic rag. The ragtime world outside the classic school was extremely variegated, and, outside of "Maple Leaf Rag," not everyone was familiar with the Stark catalogue. While Tin Pan Alley was opening new branches in the larger cities, small publishers, both rural and urban, were exercising the last vestige of pioneer initiative in publishing fine works of local talent.

The Missouri giants of course did have a great influence, especially on a second generation of ragtime composers who followed the classic rag tradition. But unless we are aware of the total spectrum of composing talent, of the variety of the ragtime expression, we have a one-dimensional view of ragtime. More important, we are missing a lot of good music. It is time to put the classic rag in proper perspective, to venture forth and embrace the rest of the ragtime world, to savor the charms of these rare ragtime jewels which have waited over a half-century to cast their syncopated spell.

The selection in *Ragtime Rediscoveries* explores the majority of the output, the rags that were being written all over America, from the early era of syncopated cakewalks on through the later fox-trot rags of the 'teens. The primary criterion used in selection was musical excellence within an overall intent to present as varied a collection as possible. Time-honored favorites too long unavailable, as well as generally unknown rags, were included to demonstrate the ebullient variety of expression in a form too often cited as stilted or stereotyped. While some of the compositions have the formality of the classic rag tradition, most are more direct, unpretentious expressions of an uncomplicated joyous spirit. Here is America at the turn of the century, syncopating from coast to coast.

N.B.: The pianist will please feel free to stomp the left foot.

II

One of the first rags to appear in print was "The Pride of Bucktown," 1897, by Robert S. Roberts, who was to become better known a few years later as an arranger for Howley, Haviland & Dresser of New York City. His more clandestine activities were the subject of a *Music Trades* article of that period, which told how Roberts was disfigured in a love-triangle quarrel while on business out of town. The publisher of this rag, Phil Kussel, was featured in a less sensational, but more important, *Music Trades* article of February 1, 1902; entitled "Phil Kussel's Retort," it was his response to one of the many anti-ragtime articles of that day: "Being in a position to feel the popular pulse, . . . and seeing the demand for both popular and so-called rag-time music, it can hardly be said that rag-time is on the wane. . . . The demand for it is really astonishing. It has not nearly reached its zenith. . . . It has been demonstrated time and time again that a poor piece of music without a good, strong theme would soon become a thing of the past. The cry of the leaders that such music is demoralizing is but a feeble attempt of the pigmy to override the giant of popular enthusiasm. It is no credit to them to decry the only thorough and truly American music."

The finest early ragtime in Cincinnati, however, was published by John Arnold. A hallmark of his publications was an extraordinarily ambitious use of syncopation. "The Amazon Rag," by Teddy Hahn, is a virtuosic early example; the broken-chord phrasing in the first strain foretells much later "novelty breaks," and the harmonies of the third strain are more involved than most writing of this early period. "Scrub Rags," by Arthur W. Mueller, is almost as surprising, abounding in "raggy" syncopations. "The Candy" is one of several excellent rags by Clarence Jones, a black conservatory-trained composer-pianist who became a novelty-ragtime master in the 1920s. He was a popular piano-roll artist on Wurlitzer's "Rolla-Artis" label, as well as on Imperial and Vocalstyle.

Although appearing here with a Cincinnati imprint, "Colonial Glide," by Paul Pratt, was originally published by J. H. Aufderheide, stockbroker and patron of later ragtime in Indianapolis. Aufderheide had originally set up business to publish the fine rags of his daughter May (her "Dusty Rag" and "Thriller Rag" are included in Dover's volume *Ragtime Rarities*). At some point in the 'teens the Mentel Brothers of Cincinnati bought the entire Aufderheide catalogue. In 1908 Pratt became manager of the J. H. Aufderheide Publishing Co., and even opened a Chicago branch office in 1911. He was a professional pit-band virtuoso pianist, playing for vaudeville acts, and a most gifted rag composer. The delightful and imaginative harmonies of "Colonial Glide" ("glide" referring to a popular dance of the day) are characteristic of creative developments within the rag form toward more variety.

"Sleepy Sidney" was probably the best of the popular lightweight Archie Scheu rags. Will B. Morrison and Cecil Duanne Crabb were both composer-publishers in Indianapolis; "Sour Grapes" has inventive, ambitious, typically Midwestern syncopations, while the arresting cover of the "Trouble" collaboration is probably by Crabb, who designed most of his covers, and who became a pioneer in outdoor advertising. The melodious "Horseshoe Rag" is by Julia Lee Niebergall, who is said to have been the actual transcriber of the Aufderheide rags—May apparently composed and played by ear.

"Campin' on de Ole Suwanee," by cakewalk writer Lee Orean Smith, was published by Vandersloot, later a prominent publisher of busy, lighthearted rags. The cover of S. M. Roberts' "Walkin' on de Rainbow Road," which seems to suggest hopes for a better tomorrow, is like a companion to that of Ben Harney's "Cakewalk in the Sky." Harney was a pioneer pianist and entertainer from Kentucky who introduced New York City to his ebullient syncopated playing in 1896 at Tony Pastor's famous emporium. His hit of that year, "Mister Johnson, Turn Me Loose," is one of the several popular "coon songs" arranged by Max Hoffman (better: Hoffmann) for his "Rag Medley" of 1897, an instrumental medley for piano published by Witmark, and one of the first syncopated publications issued in New York. Such medleys were precursors of the true rags, which were compositions of *original* syncopated melodies. (The song edition of "Mister Johnson" can be found in Dover's *Show Songs from "The Black Crook" to "The Red Mill."*) Isadore Witmark and Isaac Goldberg recalled Max Hoffman as one of the pioneer arrangers of syncopated music in their history of the House of Witmark, *From Ragtime to Swingtime*. They imply that he picked up ideas from music heard at the 1893 Chicago exposition. Hoffman was musical director of the Olympic Theatre there at the time, and mailed his arrangements to Witmark in New York. His wife was the famous vaudeville entertainer Gertrude Hoffman. The other tunes in the "Rag Medley" are:

"Good Old Wagon," another Ben Harney song of 1895 that has been called the first ragtime song ever published; "Isabelle," by Ford and Bratton; "Can't Bring Him Back," by Kollins; "Come Back My Honey," by Newcomb; "My Gal Is a High Born Lady," by Barney Fagan, one of the most popular coon-song hits of 1896 (song edition in Dover's *Song Hits from the Turn of the Century*); and the scandalous "All Coons Look Alike to Me," by black composer Ernest Hogan, the tune that caused Hogan to be ostracized by his own people for a time, though the song was simply a lament for a vanished lover.

The old Whitney-Warner Co. of Detroit later became the Remick Music Co. In both incarnations the firm issued an astounding number of popular rags. "Dixie Girl," J. B. Lampe's rousing follow-up to his phenomenal cakewalk success "Creole Belles," was popularized in a fine recording by the Van Eps Trio. J. Reginald MacEachron's "On Easy Street (In Rags)" combines ragtime and cakewalk features; it has a graceful lilt and a fine melodic flair. "Silks and Rags" is the invention of pioneer Detroit composer-bandleader Fred S. Stone, also represented in *Ragtime Rarities* by "Ma Rag Time Baby." The opening and closing sections, which comprise the "Silks," are straight Victorian waltzes, echoing the mid-nineteenth-century music of polite society; however, in the middle sections—"Rags"—Stone tears into the genteel tradition, weaving a colorful, inspired *syncopated* waltz, just as gracious and just as appropriate for elegant ballroom fetes. "Chicken Chowder" was the first hit of rag writer Irene Giblin. Its melodic chromaticism was a natural for the early Ossman-Dudley string group, who popularized it on an old Columbia 78.

Tin Pan Alley always dominated the syncopated output of New York City. As the cakewalk became a fashionable dance just before the turn of the century, publishers there flooded the market with "characteristic marches" and "cakewalk two-steps," some lightly syncopated, some just straight marches. Among this plethora of tunes which sparked an American popular-dance tradition, a few emerge as imaginative and folk-inspired. "Levee Revels: An Afro-American Cane-Hop" is one of the rare cakewalk-rag publications of 1898 (apparently a year of ferment before the boom of 1899). The composer, W. C. O'Hare, was from Shreveport, Louisiana (immortalized in Jelly Roll Morton's "Shreveport Stomp") and became a leading arranger for the Witmark Music Co. This composition enjoyed only modest success, but is one of the most inspired and soulful cakewalk-style pieces ever written. When played at a moderate tempo, the tune achieves the flavor of genuine plantation songs and dances from days beyond recall. The subtle harmonic colors, folk-style melodies and finished quality of the whole composition are much like Joplin's work to come. In fact, the "Afro-American" in the subtitle prefigures Joplin's use of it in "The Chrysanthemum: An Afro-American Intermezzo" of 1904 (in Dover's *Classic Piano Rags*). O'Hare syncopates the traditional interlude before the finale of "Levee Revels," transforming the usual "dogfight" section into a more idiomatic call and response.

Andino's "Old Virginny Barbecue" is a refreshing cakewalk score, detailed and pianistic, in contrast to many others of sparse texture. "That Scandalous Rag" is an excellent work by Edwin Kendall, who cut it on a Rythmodik piano roll, one of the all too rare occasions on which a composer recorded his own rag. "Old Virginia Rag," by Clyde Douglass, formerly of St. Louis, has no repeat signs as scored—one of the great throwaways of ragtime composition, for each strain is an inspiration, a lyrical flowing melody well worth repeating. A similar sort of understatement is the subtitle "Just Rags" on the cover of Geo. D. Barnard's "Cyclone in Darktown." The tune is one of the most ambitious adventures in ragtime, combining both bass and treble syncopations in a rousing descriptive march format.

A later ambitious experiment is "Too Much Raspberry," in the tradition of "too much" titles sparked by the success of "Too Much Mustard" in 1911. Sydney Russell's inventive, kaleidoscopic harmonies are typical of the best later ragtime. The San Francisco concern of Daniels & Russell had actually begun in St. Louis as Daniels, Russell & Boone (perhaps the legendary virtuoso pianist John W. "Blind" Boone). "Worlds Fair Rag," by Harvey M. Babcock, possibly anticipates the Panama-Pacific Exposition held in San Francisco in 1915. In a general sense, the title gives due credit to the immeasurable catalytic contribution of the various American world's fairs and expositions from 1893 on, which brought together vital ragtime talent. There are stylistic features here which parallel those in another San Francisco rag of a few years later, "Whoa! Nellie!" (in *Ragtime Rarities*), hinting at a local ragtime style. Some of these ideas were perpetuated in the incomparable playing of Paul Lingle, a West Coast ragtime and jazz pianist.

While Tin Pan Alley cranked out generally formulated rags, small-town publishers all over America were printing more folksy, individualistic works of local talent. "Cabbage-Leaf Rag" is an early tune of Les C. Copeland, an acquaintance of S. Brunson Campbell, the "Ragtime Kid" of the 1890s who studied with Scott Joplin. Both men grew up in rural Kansas. Copeland later became famous as pianist for Lew Dockstader's Minstrels, and even took his ragtime to Paris, where he ran his own cabaret. George Gershwin recalled him as one of his favorite pianists. His tunes are in a funky style typical of Midwestern folk pianists; several survive only in rare piano-roll performances. "Red Peppers" (not to be confused with Henry Lodge's "Red Pepper: A Spicy Rag") is by Imogene Giles, and a local rag of rare sensitivity and musicianship.

The total published output of New York City during the ragtime era gives only a one-dimensional view of syncopation in the East. It is not only that such Harlem piano greats as Eubie Blake, Luckey Roberts and James P. Johnson were sparsely published, because of the difficulty of their material; there were also many small publishers all over the East comparable to those further west who invested in local rags. "Rags and Tatters," by Edward Clark, Jr. of Poultney, Vermont, is a striking case in point—a rag of 1900 with the lyrical flow and folk flavor of a Mississippi Valley rag classic, in the days when Scott Joplin had scarcely been published. But why should the splendor of the New England countryside not inspire a similar lyricism?

Both Iowa and Nebraska were ragtime states. Omaha's main music publisher was A. S. Hospe, who brought out Clifford Adams' "Ink Splotch Rag," a tune that demonstrates how offbeat, in a dual sense of the term, a Midwestern folk rag could be.

Some of the most syncopated, free-wheeling folk rags were published in the southern Mississippi Valley. In 1906 Houck, of Memphis, Little Rock and other cities, issued Geraldine Dobyns' "Possum Rag," which is a quintessential example of its type: a ubiquitous style of folk-rag writing in four flats (A-flat) found throughout the Midwest and South.

The *original* Nashville sound was a distinctive folk-inspired ragtime, a bucolic hill-music flavor mixed with a flair for ambitious, "ragged" syncopations. Pioneers of this ragtime country march style were Charles Hunter and Tom Broady (in Dover's *Classic Piano Rags* and *Ragtime Rarities*), along with many "one-tune" composers working in the same area. "Why We Smile" is a less well-known but still inspired Hunter rag, while "A Coon Serenade," "Queen Raglin" and "Snowball Babe" are equally good romps in the same Tennessee vein.

The early ragtime of New Orleans frequently has the flavor of a folk song; the trio of Robert Hoffman's "Dixie Queen" of 1906 pops up in the late session (January 30, 1940) of Jelly Roll Morton and His Hot Seven as "Mama's Got a Baby (Named Tee Nah Nah)." "Tee Nah Nah" was apparently a catchy New Orleans name in the ragtime era; it appears in a dance song of J. Russell Robinson in 1912, "Te-Na-Na from New Orleans," and also as "Tee-Na-Nah: Indian Rag," by Harry Weston, a New Orleans rag of 1910. An earlier Hoffman tune, "A Dingy Slowdown" of 1900, is a polished score for early New Orleans ragtime, and contrasts with several other less successfully written efforts there at the turn of the century. The Robert Hoffman rags, steeped in local folk roots, preserve a background flavor of New Orleans music which jazz giants such as Jelly Roll Morton would absorb into their own creations later on.

A. Maggio's "I Got the Blues" of 1908 is certainly one of the earliest published experiments with blues composition. This mix of rag and blues was not peculiar to New

Orleans, but pops up even earlier in St. Louis (see the first strain of Chapman and Smith's "One o' Them Things!" in *Ragtime Rarities*) and was characteristic of folk playing in the Mississippi Valley. Here Maggio uses twelve-bar blues in G, followed by a section in parallel minor (G minor) and ending with an ancient folk-rag riff, making the "blues" rather ambivalent, but fascinating.

Cincinnati-born Joe Jordan enjoyed a long and profitable career as both composer and arranger. His earliest musical period was spent with Tom Turpin and the Rosebud Bar group of musicians in St. Louis. Unlike most pianists who remained there until after the 1904 World's Fair, Jordan left in 1903 for Chicago, where he wrote and directed the music for the Pekin Theatre, a successful black theater operation much like the Turpin Brothers' later Booker T. Washington Theatre in St. Louis. Jordan's early rags sound as if they had been written at the Rosebud with Tom Turpin looking over his shoulder. His "J. J. J. Rag" of 1905, also known as "Three J Rag," involves two other St. Louis pianists. The first strain is identical to the first one of "Delmar Rag," by ragtime virtuoso Charley Thompson. During the early 1960s, when both Jordan and Thompson were recruited for Bob Darch's *Reunion in Ragtime* recording project, they set the record straight by crediting the theme to still another legendary St. Louis ragtimer, Conroy Casey, whom Charley also remembered as one of Scott Joplin's favorite pianists.

Cy Seymour is a mystery (perhaps another ragtime alias?), but the rags that bear his name are all excellent without exception. His most popular was "Panama Rag" of 1904 (not the same as the jazz classic "Panama," by Will Tyers). "Holy Moses" is perhaps Seymour's most melodious rag. Bess Rudisill, a St. Louis pianist-composer, wrote an intriguing descriptive rag in "The Eight O'Clock Rush," using eccentric syncopations and bass rumblings to suggest the sounds of the hectic early morning hours.

In 1902 the obscure Medbery Music Co. of Chicago issued Harry W. Jones's "Swamptown Shuffle," an inspired cakewalk that captures an authentic folk-roots flavor, in which the early "breakdowns" and marches can be heard evolving into syncopation.

W. C. Powell was the pen name of Chicago-based composer W. C. Polla. The cover of "Funny Folks" of 1904 depicts the heterogeneity of the St. Louis World's Fair, with its delineation of foreign types in silhouette against typical urban fairground buildings.

"The Cannon Ball," by the mysterious Jos. C. Northup (not to be confused with another pioneer ragtime arranger/composer working in Chicago, Theodore Northrup), became one of the most popular rags of all time. Its pianistic opening strain was probably a popular floating folk-rag theme; it appears in slightly modified form in two earlier rags, "Levee Rag," by Mullen (1902), and "Easy Money: A Ragtime Sonata," "coined by" A. H.

Tournade, a New Orleans rag of 1904. The arranger of "The Cannon Ball," Thomas R. Confare, probably had a heavy hand in the tune, as he collaborated on a sequel with Morris Silver in 1909, "Bombshell Rag."

The cover text of H. H. Mincer's 1899 "Virginia Two-Step," which adds the words "& Hot Rag Swing," reveals how early "hot" and "swing" were associated with syncopated music. This piece was rediscovered in the 1960s by the fine ragtime pianist Robert Ackerman, who will play it at the drop of a hat.

"Rag Alley Dream," by Mattie Harl Burgess, evokes an informal cakewalk on a back street, a rather common pastime in the late 1890s and early 1900s. The trio has a heavier piano texture than the first two strains, and finishes the tune in a strutting folk-rag style.

"Policy King" was the most successful cakewalk of C. B. Brown, and remained popular as late as 1919, when the great banjoist Fred Van Eps recorded it.

In his later years, Brun Campbell, mentioned above in connection with Copeland, recalled both "Rags to Burn" and its composer, Frank X. McFadden, in one of his many published ragtime reminiscences. The medley by this "peerless ragtime pianist" is a loose compilation of early Kansas/Missouri folk-ragtime strains. Several are rather eccentric and idiosyncratic, and must reflect much of the ragtime playing in the earliest years. Campbell incorporated parts of this medley into his own tunes, most notably "Chestnut St. in the '90s" (probably his best solo and still regrettably unavailable in reissue) and "Ginger Snap Rag," reissued on one of two Euphonic LPs by Campbell historian and collector Paul Affeldt. Dozens of fine rags were published in Kansas City by Jenkins and other smaller concerns, from 1899 on. Colburn's "Dimples" and Cozad's "Eatin' Time" are memorable contributions by local writers.

Missouri classic-rag composer James Scott published in Kansas City as well as St. Louis. "Dixie Dimples," issued by Livernash in Kansas City, is probably Scott's most obscure composition. The tune is a beautiful addition to the late foxtrot rag genre of the 'teens. Two Scott classic rags, published in St. Louis, are included here. They are vital works, too long unavailable. "Ophelia Rag" begins in a lusty vein, harking back to the early days of folk ragtime (the chromatic treble run in the first strain is identical to one in Turpin's "Rag-Time Nightmare" of 1900—in *Classic Piano Rags*); the trio, however, is more involved, with abrupt, motivic phrasing, foretelling later Scott complexities. The cover of "Ophelia Rag" is from a once popular comic strip by Clair Victor Dwiggins, who did other work for the publisher Stark (see Scott's "Ragtime Betty" in *Classic Piano Rags*.) "Princess Rag" is a lighthearted Scott work which alternates his short phrasing with the longer, lyrical lines of the trio. The cover picture is signed "R. Scott," who may have been a relative of the composer. The title, if it is Scott's, may refer to the Princess Theatre in Aurora, Mo., in the composer's home territory; it is more probable that publisher Stark titled the rag (as he did many of Scott's) after a St. Louis theater of the same name that featured ragtime.

Balmer & Weber, St. Louis' oldest music publishing house, and the first west of the Mississippi, originally brought out E. Warren Furry's "Robardina Rag" in 1902. It was then bought and published during the World's Fair of 1904 by the Thiebes-Stierlin Co. The tune has the character of the early Rosebud Bar rags of Tom Turpin and Joe Jordan. Another with much the same flavor is "Slivers," by Harry L. Cook, better known as the professional clown Slivers. Cook later worked with the Six Brown Brothers, a popular saxophone group who recorded for Victor in the 'teens. His "Shovel Fish" of 1907 is an inspired medley of six contrasting folk strains, ingeniously arranged so that the rag achieves a great unity.

Charles Humfeld, known as "Humpy," and more pretentiously as "the Musical Architect," penned several good rags. His best was "Who Let the Cows Out?: A Bully Rag," which challenges the pianist in a one-bar break to "Make a noise like a cow," undoubtedly once a local vaudeville feature.

The Stark press, which published the two above-mentioned James Scott pieces, also supplemented its classic-rag catalogue with a variety of other works that included cakewalks, folk rags and even latterday foxtrot rags. Stark may not have accepted jazz, but he championed the rag up through and beyond the final years of the ragtime era, and even contributed to later developments within the form.

"Trombone Johnsen" of 1902, advertised as one that "tells the artistic story with a smile," was in the popular march-cakewalk format of tunes which were generally played by (and written for) bands showcasing the slide trombone. Perhaps the most gifted artist of this genre was the trombone virtuoso Arthur Pryor of St. Joseph, Missouri. Once featured with Sousa's band, he went on to form his own orchestra, which became popular on Victor Records. The very title of his biggest hit, "Razzazza Mazzazza" (published by Carl Fisher), is almost onomatopoetic, suggesting typically raucous trombone smears.

Etilmon J. Stark, the writer of "Trombone Johnsen," was the eldest son of publisher John Stark, and a prolific composer and arranger (he did most of the orchestral Red Back Book arrangements). His fine "Gum Shoe" is in the bouncing foxtrot rhythm of the 'teens—a striking development from the older cakewalk/two-step style of "Trombone Johnson." His haunting "Billiken Rag" of 1913 was advertised as "picture show, first scene," suggesting its use for accompanying silent movies. Traditionally an Oriental good-luck charm, the "Billiken" also celebrates a local St. Louis club, and is today still the name of St. Louis University's basketball club.

There is a strong cakewalk feeling in Catlin's "Sympathetic Jasper: A Drag Rag" of 1905, referring to the slow-drag dance step of the day. Stark's blurb for this one was elaborate: "Chicago here throws its line into the stream with a bait for popular approval. Jasper is sympathetic all right, and as might be expected from a Chicago union musician, is also intelligent and snappy . . . the name pipes its quality to a hair's breadth."

"The Calla Lily Rag," by Logan Thane (or Nat E. Solomons—the alias on the title page looks almost like a joint credit inside), is one of several forgotten but captivating excursions into the legato classic-rag style that Stark must have encouraged in his composers.

"The Checkerboard" of 1914 is a shining example of the many excellent forgotten gems of ragtime. It was popular briefly in an old QRS piano-roll version.

"Moonshine Rag" of 1916 is the folksy, pianistic conception of one Edward Hudson, who wrote rags for Stark on into the early 1920s. It is spiced with a walking-bass figure, a popular feature of ragtime performance from the earliest days. This rag probably celebrates the Moonshine Gardens, a St. Louis club in which classic rag composer Arthur Marshall played late in his career (see *Rags and Ragtime*, by David A. Jasen and Trebor Tichenor).

Anderson's "Keystone Rag" is a rare survival from the last fading years of the Stark press. As finances grew slimmer, Stark published the tunes with less elaborate covers, frequently reusing a single cover plate for two or more compositions, and often did not even bother to copyright the works. In the last years of ragtime, instrumental-music output was geared generally to an American public gone dance-crazy. Foxtrot rags were written with a jaunty dotted-note rhythm that suggested the triplet feeling of the jazz swing to come. The rag form in these years became a fascinating hybrid, taking on early-jazz and blues coloration, with an expanding harmonic palette.

The incredibly rare "Keystone Rag" comes from the collection of pioneer ragtime and jazz historian William Russell. When he bought it from William P. Stark in the 1940s, he was informed that the composer, Willie Anderson, was a black writer. The tune could celebrate either the popular Keystone silent films or a prominent local hotel in the old Chestnut Valley district. "Keystone Rag" is a miniature masterpiece, a composition from the twilight days of ragtime with echoes of the old school—a lyrical, wistful farewell to the days of the gracious, elegant rags. A grand era was over, the pioneer publishers were finished. The great ragtime pianists were vanishing. But the great rags they all so lovingly composed and published will live forever as unquestionably one of our richest musical heritages.

N.B.: "These rags will add materially to the gaiety of nations," John S. Stark.

CONTENTS

Publisher, city and date are in parentheses.

Clifford Adams   *page*

     INK SPLOTCH RAG (A. Hospe Co., Omaha, 1909)   1

Willie Anderson

     KEYSTONE [KEY-STONE] RAG (Stark Music Co., St. Louis, 1921)   6

J. E. Andino

     OLE VIRGINNY BARBECUE (Andino & Ruehl, New York, 1899)   9

Harvey M. Babcock

     WORLDS FAIR RAG (Harvey M. Babcock, San Francisco, 1912)   14

George D. Barnard

     A CYCLONE IN DARKTOWN (Carl Fischer, New York, 1910)   18

Charles B. Brown

     POLICY KING (Will Rossiter, Chicago, 1905)   23

Mattie Harl Burgess

     RAG-ALLEY DREAM (Will Rossiter, Chicago, 1902)   28

E. L. Catlin

     SYMPATHETIC JASPER (John Stark & Son, St. Louis, 1905)   33

Edward Clark, Jr.

     RAGS AND TATTERS (Edward Clark, Jr., Poultney, Vt., 1900)   37

L. E. Colburn

     DIMPLES (Colburn-Rendina Music Publishing Co., Kansas City, Mo., 1910)   41

Harry L. Cook

     THE SHOVEL FISH (Jerome H. Remick & Co., Detroit, 1907, 1908)   46
     SLIVERS (Central Music Co., St. Louis, 1909)   51

Les Copeland

     CABBAGE-LEAF RAG (Marsh & Needles Music Publishing Co.,
         Wichita, 1909)   56

Irene Cozad

     EATIN' TIME (J. W. Jenkins' Sons Music Co., Kansas City, Mo., 1913)   59

Geraldine Dobyns

     POSSUM RAG (O. K. Houck Piano Co., Memphis, 1907   64

Clyde Douglass

     OLD VIRGINIA RAG (Parker Music Co., New York, 1907)   70

page

C. Roland Flick
SNOWBALL BABE (Frank G. Fite, Nashville, 1900)   75

E. Warren Furry
THE ROBARDINA RAG (Balmer & Weber Music House Co., St. Louis, 1902)
[preceded by the cover, only, of the 1904 Thiebes-Stierlin edition]   80

Irene M. Giblin
CHICKEN CHOWDER (Jerome H. Remick & Co., New York, 1905)   86

Imogene Giles
RED PEPPERS (Giles Bros., Quincy, Ill., 1907)   91

Teddy Hahn
THE AMAZON RAG (Miller-Arnold Publishing Co., Cincinnati, 1904)   96

A. E. Henrich
QUEEN RAGLIN [RAGLAN] (H. A. French, Nashville, 1902)   100

Bob Hoffman
A DINGY SLOWDOWN (Duggan-Hoffman, New Orleans, 1900)   105
DIXIE QUEEN (Victor Kremer Co., Chicago, 1906, 1907)   110

Max Hoffman[n]
RAG MEDLEY (M. Witmark & Sons, New York, 1897)   115

Edward Hudson
MOONSHINE RAG (Stark Music Co., St. Louis, 1916)   121

Charles Humfeld
WHO LET THE COWS OUT? (Howard & Browne Music Co., St. Louis, 1910)   126

Charles Hunter
WHY WE SMILE (Frank G. Fite, Nashville, 1903)   131

M. H. Irish
A COON SERENADE (Frank G. Fite, Nashville, 1903)   135

Elijah W. Jimerson [Jamerson?]
THE CHECKERBOARD (Syndicate Music Co., St. Louis, 1914)   139

Clarence Jones
THE CANDY (John Arnold, Cincinnati, 1909)   144

Harry W. Jones
SWAMPTOWN SHUFFLE (Medbery Music Co., Chicago, 1902)   149

Joe Jordan
J. J. J. RAG (Pekin Pub. Co.. Chicago, 1905) [cover missing]   153

Edwin F. Kendall
THAT SCANDALOUS RAG (John Franklin Music Co., New York, 1912)   156

J. Bodewalt Lampe
DIXIE GIRL (Whitney-Warner Publishing Co., Detroit, 1903)   161

J. Reginald MacEachron *page*

    ON EASY STREET (IN RAGS) (Whitney-Warner Publishing Co., Detroit, 1901, 1902)   166

A. Maggio

    I GOT THE BLUES (A. Maggio, New Orleans, 1908)   171

Frank X. McFadden

    RAGS TO BURN (J. W. Jenkins' Sons Music Co., Kansas City, Mo., 1899)   174

Harry H. Mincer

    VIRGINIA TWO-STEP (Windsor Music Co., Chicago, 1899)   181

Will B. Morrison

    SOUR GRAPES ("Morrison," Indianapolis, 1912)   185

Will B. Morrison & Cecil Duanne Crabb

    TROUBLE (Mentel Bros. Publishing Co., Cincinnati, 1914)   190

Arthur W. Mueller

    SCRUB RAGS (Arnold Pub. Co., Cincinnati, 1904)   194

Julia Lee Niebergall

    HORSESHOE RAG (J. H. Aufderheide & Co., Indianapolis, 1911)   199

Jos. C. Northup

    THE CANNON BALL (Victor Kremer Co., Chicago, 1905)   203

William Christopher O'Hare

    LEVEE REVELS (M. Witmark & Sons, New York, 1898)   209

W. C. Powell [Polla]

    FUNNY FOLKS (W. C. Polla Co., Chicago, 1904)   214

Paul Pratt

    COLONIAL GLIDE (Mentel Bros. Publishing Co., Cincinnati, 1914)   218

Arthur Pryor

    RAZZAZZA MAZZAZZA (Carl Fischer, New York, 1906)   223

Robert S. Roberts

    THE PRIDE OF BUCKTOWN (Philip Kussel, Cincinnati, 1897)   227

S. M. Roberts

    WALKIN' ON DE RAINBOW ROAD (M. D. Swisher, Philadelphia, 1899)   231

Bess E. Rudisill

    THE EIGHT O'CLOCK RUSH (Sear-Wilson Music Publishing Co., Chicago, 1911)   235

Sydney K. Russell

    TOO MUCH RASPBERRY (Charles N. Daniels, San Francisco, 1916)   239

Archie W. Scheu

    SLEEPY SIDNEY (A. W. Scheu Music Pub. Co., Cincinnati, 1907)   243

James Scott   *page*

OPHELIA RAG (Stark Music Co., St. Louis, 1910)   247
PRINCESS RAG (Stark Music Co., St. Louis, 1911)   252
DIXIE DIMPLES (Will L. Livernash Music Co., Kansas City, Mo., 1918)   256

Cy Seymour

PANAMA RAG (Albright Music Co., Chicago, 1904)   259
HOLY MOSES (Arnett-Delonais Co., Chicago, 1906)   264

Lee Orean Smith

CAMPIN' ON DE OLE SUWANEE (Vandersloot Music Co., Williamsport,
    Pa., 1899)   268

E. J. Stark

TROMBONE JOHNSEN (John Stark & Sons, St. Louis, 1902)   272
BILLIKEN RAG (Stark Music Co., St. Louis, 1913)   277
GUM SHOE (Stark Music Co., St. Louis, 1917)   282

Fred S. Stone

SILKS AND RAGS (Whitney-Warner Publishing Co., Detroit, 1901)   285

Logan Thane [and/or Nat E. Solomons?]

CALLA LILY RAG (Stark Music Co., St. Louis, 1907)   292

RAGTIME
REDISCOVERIES

To my Friend C. F. Huffman.

INK SPLOTCH RAG.

A Rag Time Splash.

CLIFFORD ADAMS.

TRIO.

KEYSTONE

RAG

Music by
WILLIE ANDERSON

STARK MUSIC CO.
ST LOUIS, MO.

Key-Stone

RAG

Moderato

By WILLIE ANDERSON

7

OLE VIRGINNY

A CHARACTERISTIC MARCH AND CAKE WALK

BARBECUE

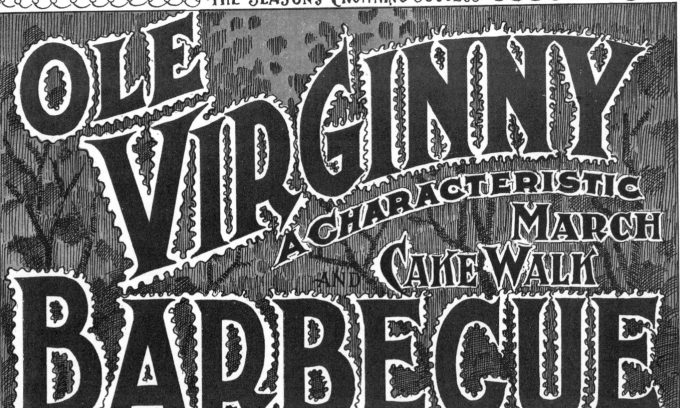

5

By J. E. ANDINO.

PUBLISHED BY
ANDINO & RUEHL
SIXTH AVE & 15TH ST.
~ NEW YORK ~

GUCKERT MUSIC PUB. CO.
BAND
ORCHESTRA
MANDOLIN
GUITAR
ZITHER
ARRANGE
MENTS

SELLING AGENTS
ENTERPRISE MUSIC SUPPLY CO.
30 W. 29 ST
NEW YORK CITY.

OLE VIRGINNY BARBECUE.

Characteristic March and Cake Walk.

by J. E. ANDINO.

Allegro moderato.

Trio.

WORLDS FAIR RAG

Grace Purvis,
497 Golden Gate Ave.,
San Francisco, Cal.

HARVEY M. BABCOCK
SAN FRANCISCO CAL

Worlds Fair Rag.

Not too fast.

By **HARVEY M. BABCOCK.**

Trio.

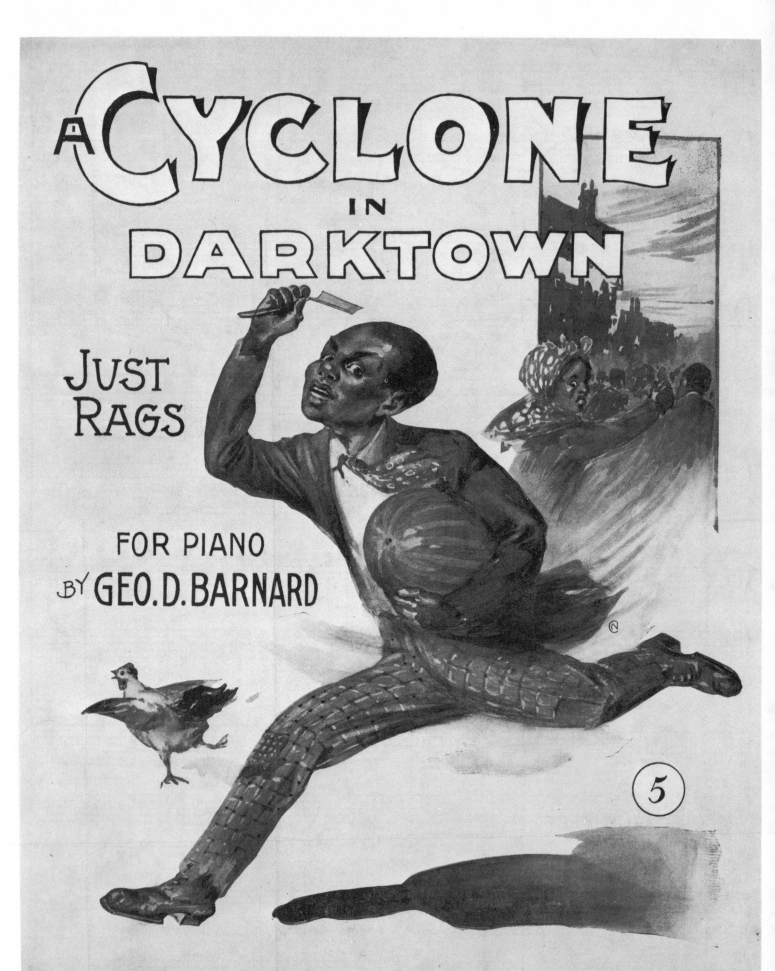

A Cyclone in Darktown

Just Rag

Geo. D Barnard

Trio

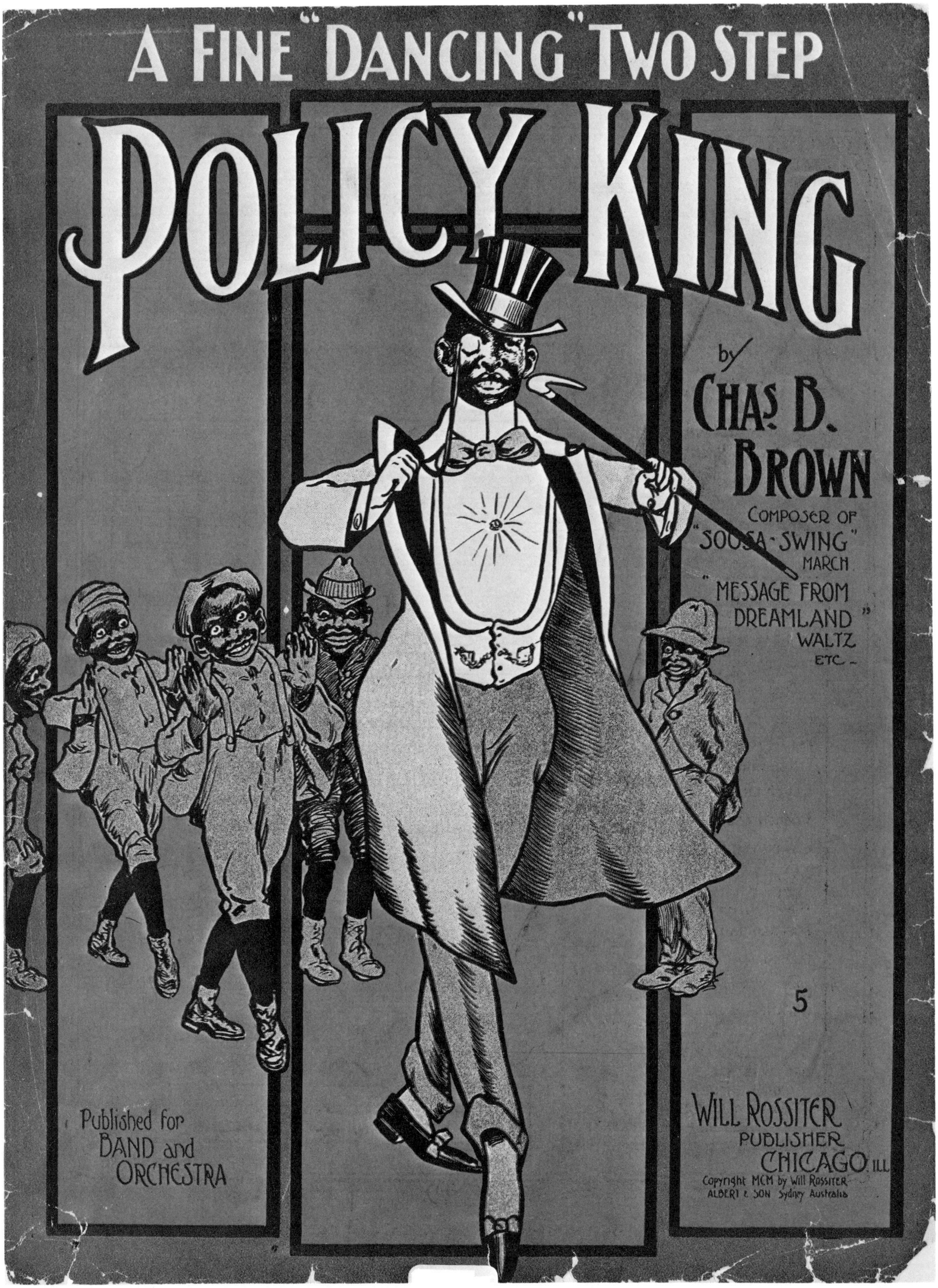

A FINE "DANCING" TWO STEP
POLICY KING
by
CHAS. B. BROWN
COMPOSER OF
"SOUSA-SWING" MARCH
"MESSAGE FROM DREAMLAND" WALTZ
ETC.
5
Published for BAND and ORCHESTRA
WILL ROSSITER
PUBLISHER
CHICAGO. ILL
Copyright MCM by Will Rossiter
ALBERT & SON Sydney Australia

POLICY KING.
A Popular Two Step.

By CHAS. B. BROWN.

RAG ALLEY DREAM

ROBT. BURGESS

BY

MATTIE HARL BURGESS

PUBLISHED FOR BAND & ORCHESTRA

WILL ROSSITER
PUBLISHER
56 5TH AVENUE, CHICAGO.

5

RAG-ALLEY DREAM.

By Mattie Harl Burgess.

TRIO

mf

Sympathetic Jasper.

A Drag Rag.

E. L. CATLIN.

INTRO.
Moderato.

Slowly.

TRIO.

RAGS AND TATTERS

March and Two Step.

By EDWARD CLARK, JR

5

Published by
EDWARD CLARK, JR
POULTNEY, VT.

RAGS AND TATTERS.
MARCH.

EDWARD CLARK Jr.

Dimples

RAG TIME INTERMEZZO

5

BY

L. E. COLBURN

COMPOSER OF
FOXY GRANDPA SCHOTTISCHE
FOXY KID SCHOTTISCHE

PUBLISHED
BY
COLBURN-RENDINA
MUSIC PUBLISHING CO
KANSAS CITY~MO

"DIMPLES"

RAG TIME INTERMEZZO.

By L. E. COLBURN.

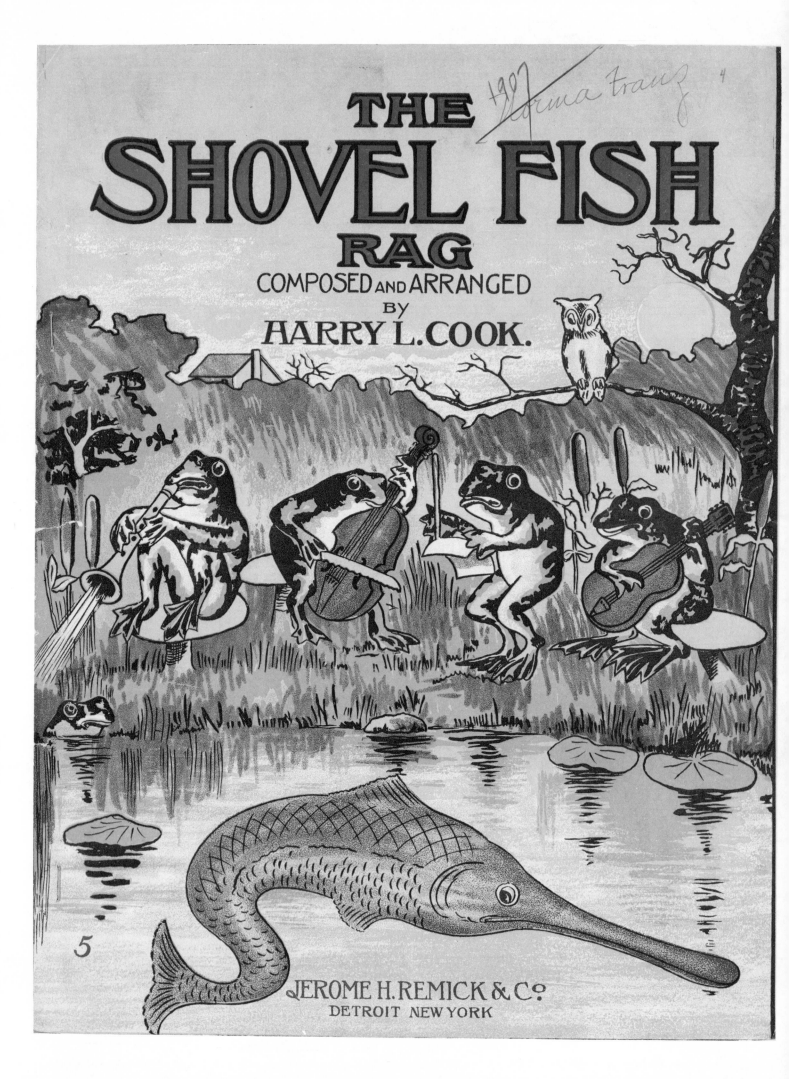

The Shovel Fish.
RAG.

Slow Drag.

HARRY L. COOK.

1st and 2d times.

3d time.

Fine.

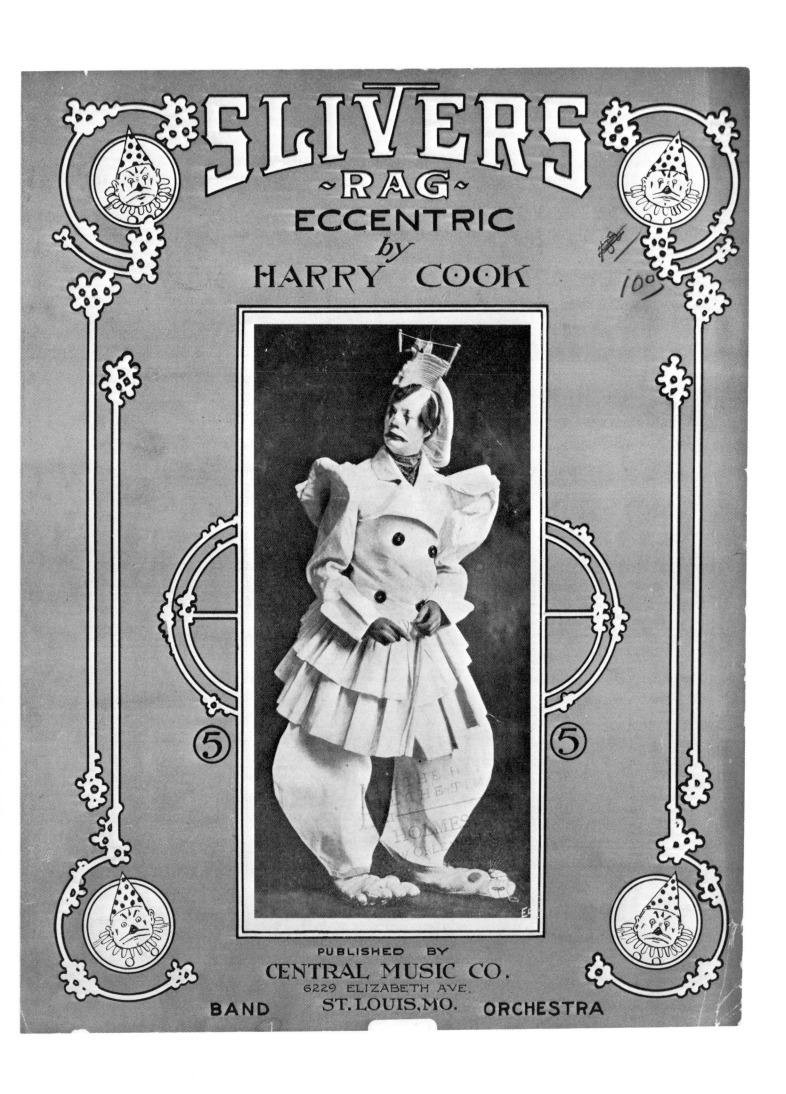

"SLIVERS."

ECCENTRIC RAG.

As used by "SLIVERS" in his famous Pantomine,
"THE BALL GAME."

HARRY COOK.

Slow Drag. S-L-O-W.

CABBAGE-LEAF
RAG

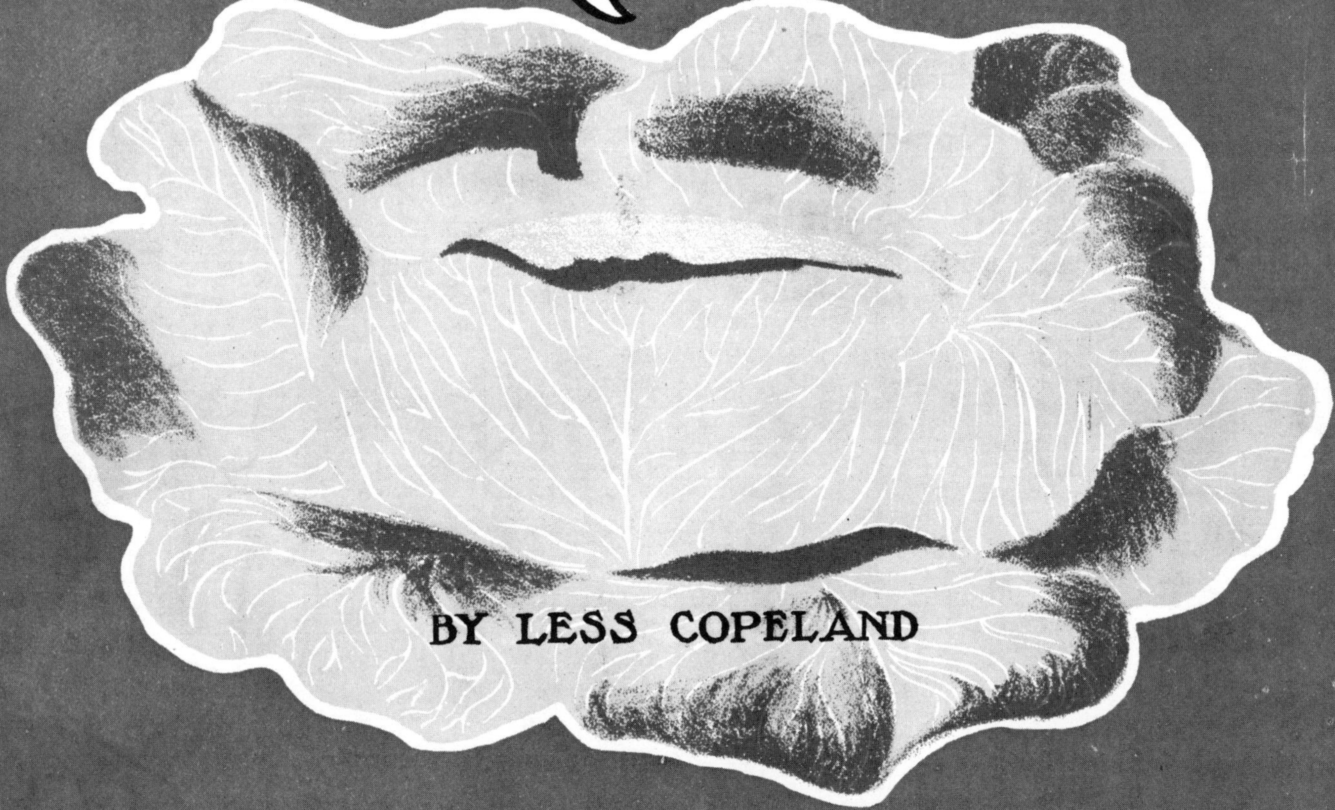

BY LESS COPELAND

A SUPERB RAGGED MELODY

A Rich Two-Step

5

MARSH & NEEDLES
MUSIC PUBLISHING CO
WICHITA, KANSAS.

Cabbage-Leaf Rag.

By LESS COPELAND.

EATIN'-TIME RAG

PIANO

By
IRENE COZAD
composer of
"AFFINITY
RAG"

5

"Ragtime Bob" MARCH

W. E. PARKER

J. W. Jenkins Son's Music Co.

PUBLISHERS
KANSAS CITY, Mo.

N. Y. TITLE-PAGE CO.

EATIN' TIME

Rag

IRENE COZAD

TRIO

Respectfully dedicated to MR. F. E. MILES

427

Possum Rag

COMPOSED BY
GERALDINE DOBYNS

PUBLISHED BY
O. K. HOUCK PIANO CO.
MEMPHIS — ST. LOUIS — NASHVILLE
CHATTANOOGA — LITTLE ROCK
COPYRIGHT MCMVII BY GERALDINE DOBYNS.

Price 50

POSSUM RAG.

Composed by GERALDINE DOBYNS

Old Virginia Rag.
March and Two-Step
"Ragtime Bob" Darch
P.O. BOX 323, VIRGINIA CITY, NEV.
By Clyde Douglass
PARKER MUSIC COMPANY, 110 W. 40th St., NEW YORK.
CHAS. SHEARD & Co. London, Eng. CANADIAN AMERICAN MUSIC Co. Toronto.
5

Old Virginia Rag.

March & Two Step.

CLYDE DOUGLASS.

Trio.

Snowball Babe

A Rag Time Inspiration

5

"ABE" THE COAL MAN.

C Roland Flick

PUBLISHED BY
FRANK G. FITE
NASHVILLE, TENN.

SNOWBALL BABE.

C. ROLAND FLICK.

76

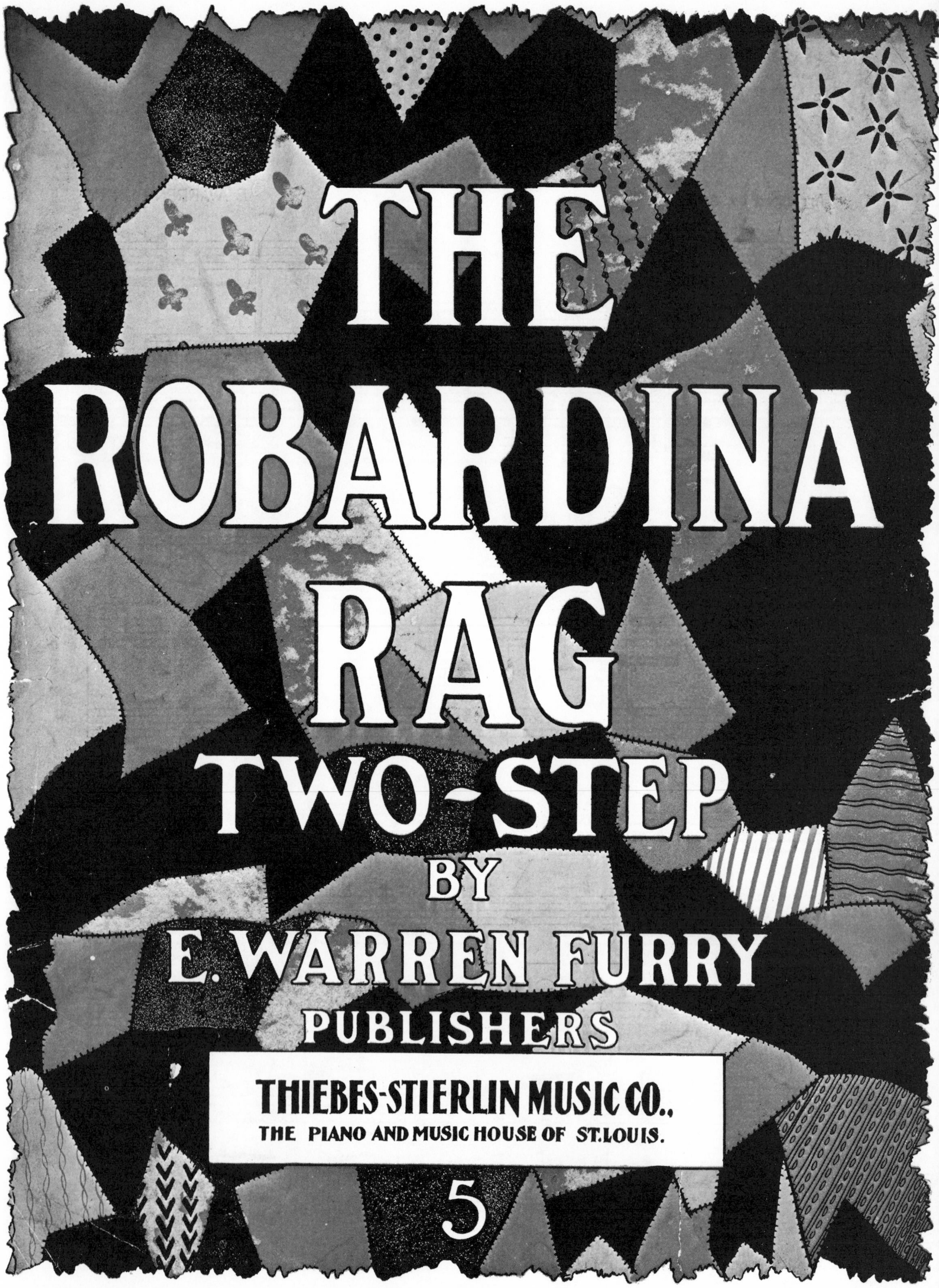

THE ROBARDINA RAG

TWO-STEP

BY
E. WARREN FURRY

PUBLISHERS

THIEBES-STIERLIN MUSIC CO.,
THE PIANO AND MUSIC HOUSE OF ST. LOUIS.

5

DEDICATED TO
MISS LUCY KENNEY,
ST. LOUIS, MO.

THE

ROBARDINA RAG~

TWO-STEP.

5

"Ragtime Bob" DARCH
P.O. BOX 328, VIRGINIA CITY, NEV.

COMPOSED BY

E. WARREN
FURRY.

PUBLISHED BY
BALMER & WEBER MUSIC HOUSE CO.
ST. LOUIS, MO.

ROBARDINA RAG.

Composed by . . . . E. WARREN FURRY.

Arranged by Arthur B. Mooney.

Piano

CHICKEN CHOWDER
CHARACTERISTIC TWO-STEP BY IRENE GIBLIN
GENE BUCK
JEROME H. REMICK & CO NEW-YORK WHITNEY WARNER PUB. CO. DETROIT

CHICKEN CHOWDER.
Characteristic Two Step.

IRENE M. GIBLIN.

88 *Irene M. Giblin*

Fine.

RED PEPPERS

Two-Step

By

Imogene Giles

5

PUBLISHED BY
GILES BROS.
QUINCY, ILL.

RED PEPPERS
TWO STEP

IMOGENE GILES

Moderato

Trio

Dedicated to Amazon Canoe Club.

THE AMAZON RAG

Two Step.

by Teddy Hahn.

⑤

Miller-Arnold Publishing Co.
127 West Fourth Street, CINCINNATI, O.

The Amazon Rag.

by Teddy Hahn.

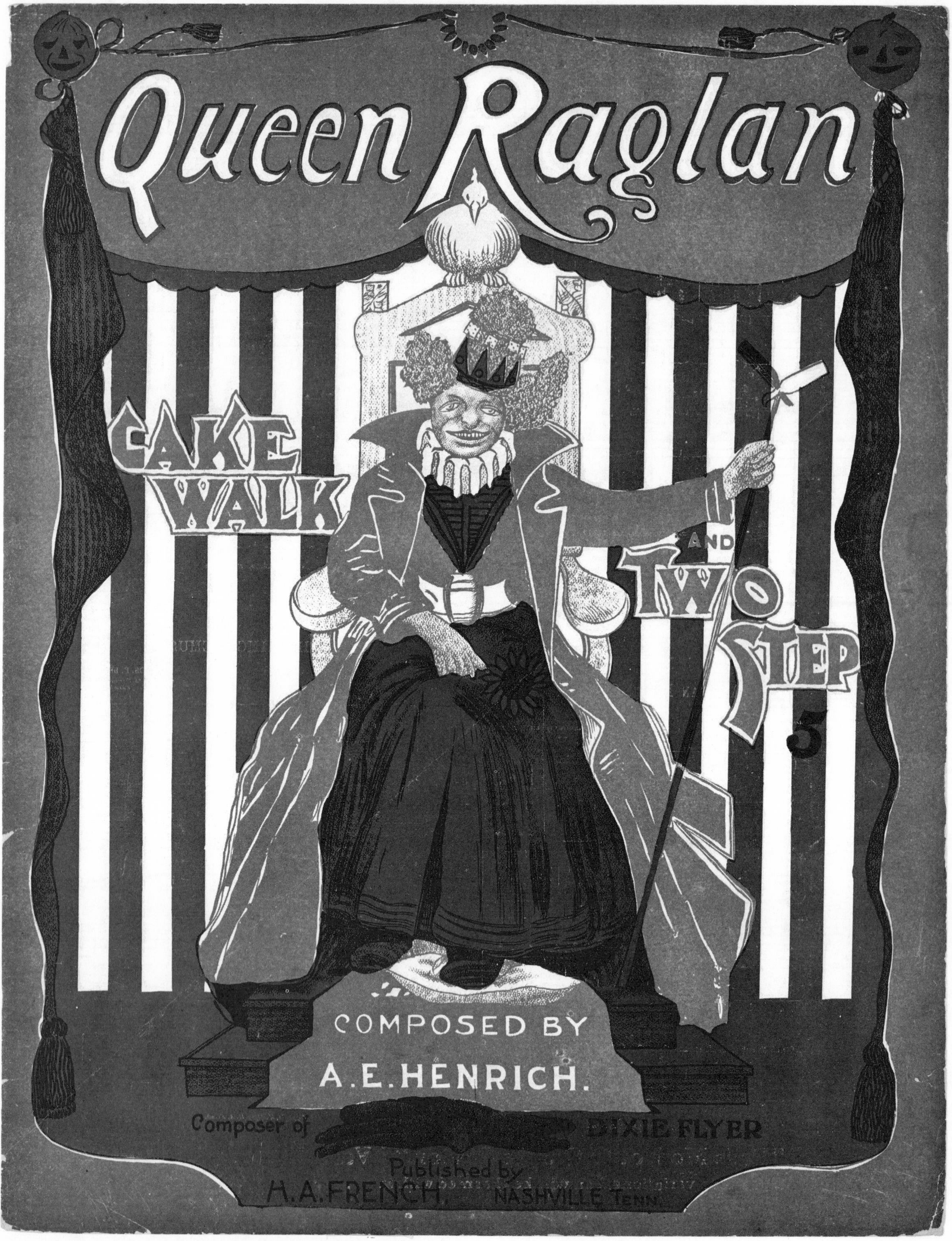

Queen Raglan

CAKE WALK

AND TWO STEP

5

COMPOSED BY

A. E. HENRICH.

Composer of DIXIE FLYER

Published by

H. A. FRENCH, NASHVILLE Tenn.

Queen Raglin.
Two Step.

A. E. HENRICH.

104   A. E. Henrich

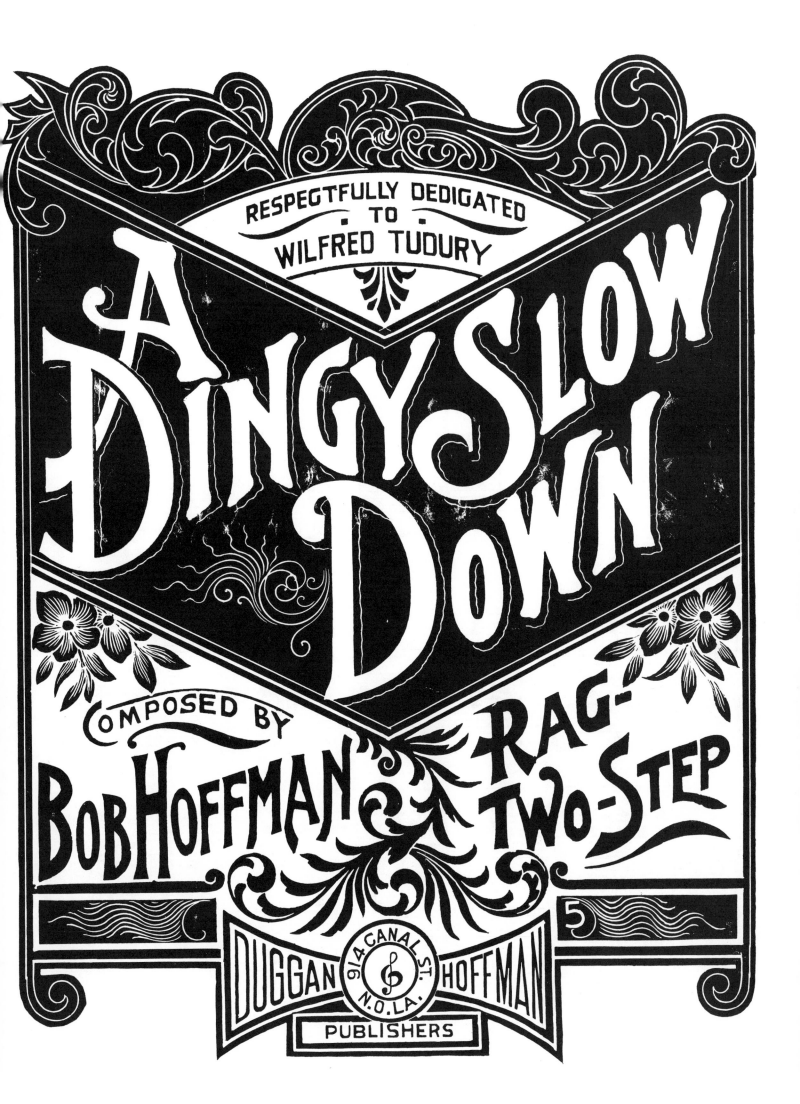

A Dingy Slowdown.

BOB HOFFMAN.

DIXIE QUEEN
By ROBERT HOFFMAN
A SOUTHERN RAGTIME
5
VICTOR KREMER CO. CHICAGO, NEW YORK, LONDON, SYDNEY

DIXIE QUEEN.

By BOB HOFFMAN.

111

THE PRESENT DAY FAD.

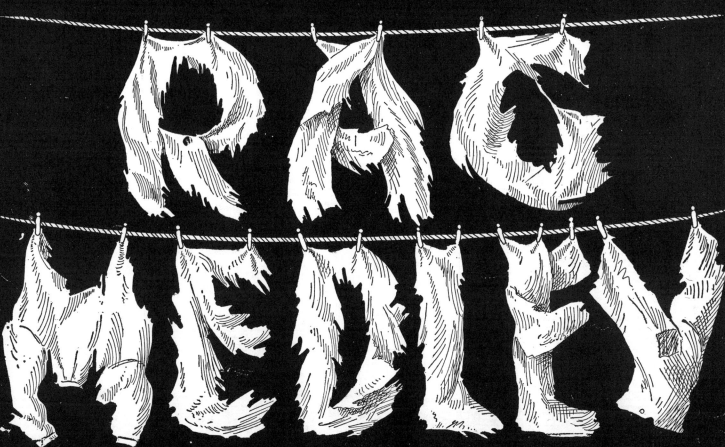

RAG MEDLEY

SPECIALLY ARRANGED FOR PIANO ON THE

WITMARK POPULAR PUBLICATIONS
"GOOD OLD WAGON" "ISABELLE." "MY GAL IS A HIGH BORN LADY."
"COME BACK MY HONEY I'SE BEEN WAITIN'." "CAN'T BRING HIM BACK".
"MR. JOHNSON TURN ME LOOSE." "ALL COONS LOOK ALIKE TO ME".

by MAX HOFFMAN.

PUBLISHED BY

NEW YORK.
49-51 W. 28TH. STREET.
M. WITMARK & SONS
CHICAGO.
SCHILLER THEATRE BLD'G.

LONDON ENG.
CHAS. SHEARD & CO.
TORONTO. CAN.
WHALEY ROYCE & CO.

RAG MEDLEY.

Arr. by MAX HOFFMANN

(Good old wagon.)

(Ford & Bratton) Isabelle.

.Can't bring him back. (Kollins)

Come back my honey. (Newcomb)

Slow.

My Gal is a high born lady. (Fagan)

Mister Johnson (Harney)

Legato

118 Max Hoffman

All Coons (Hogan)

MOONSHINE RAG
BY EDWARD HUDSON
Irebor Jay Tichenor
STARK MUSIC CO
ST. LOUIS, MO.

Moonshine Rag

EDWARD HUDSON

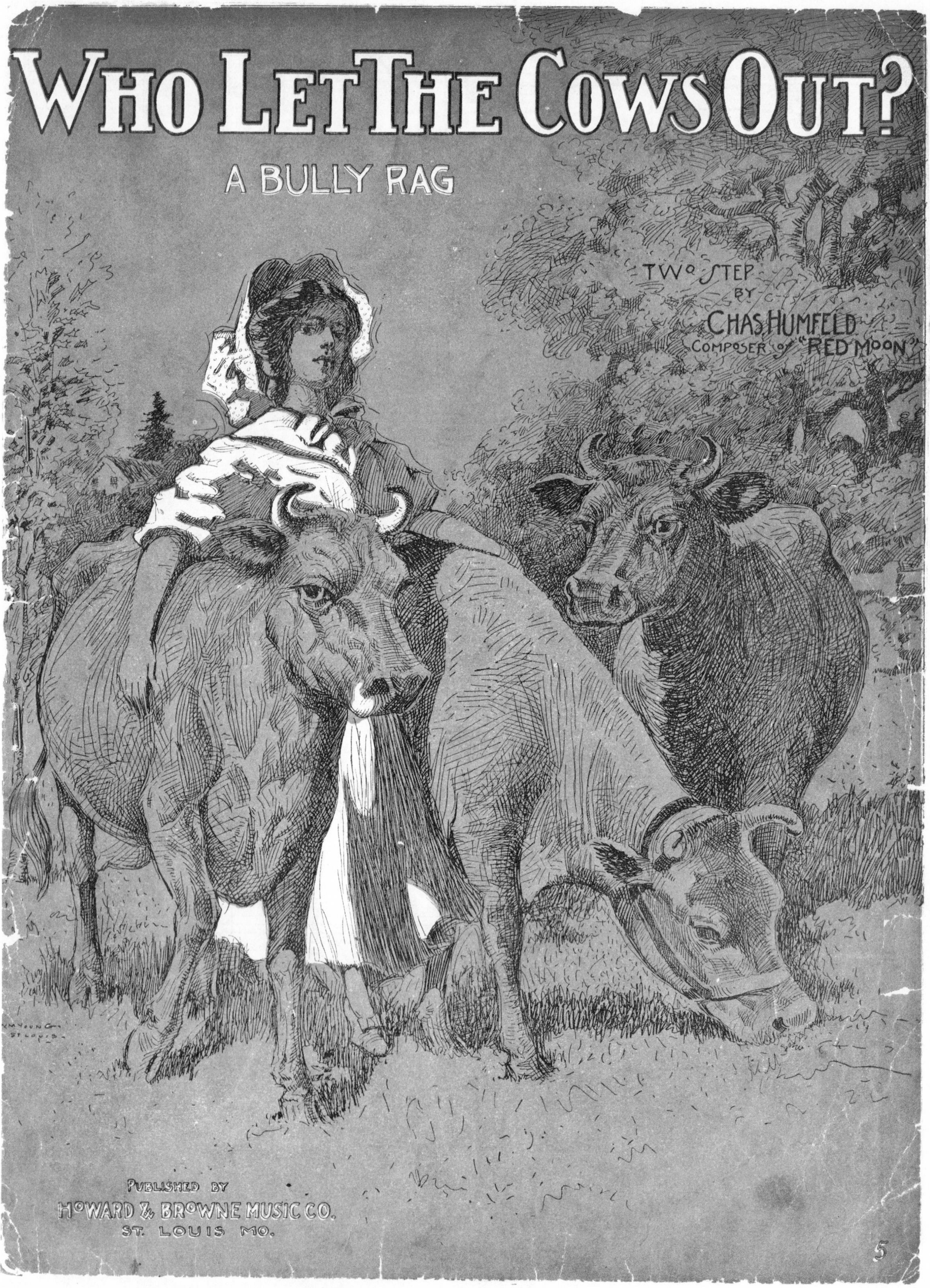

Who Let The Cows Out?

A BULLY RAG

TWO STEP
BY
CHAS HUMFELD
COMPOSER OF "RED MOON"

PUBLISHED BY
HOWARD & BROWNE MUSIC CO.
ST. LOUIS MO.

5

Respectfully dedicated to Josef. Fuchs.

WHO LET THE COWS OUT?

A BULLY RAG.

CHAS. HUMFELD.
Composer of "RED MOON" etc.

Tempo di Rag-etta Slow-vere.

Make a noise
like a cow.

Oh!you cowl!

Why We Smile

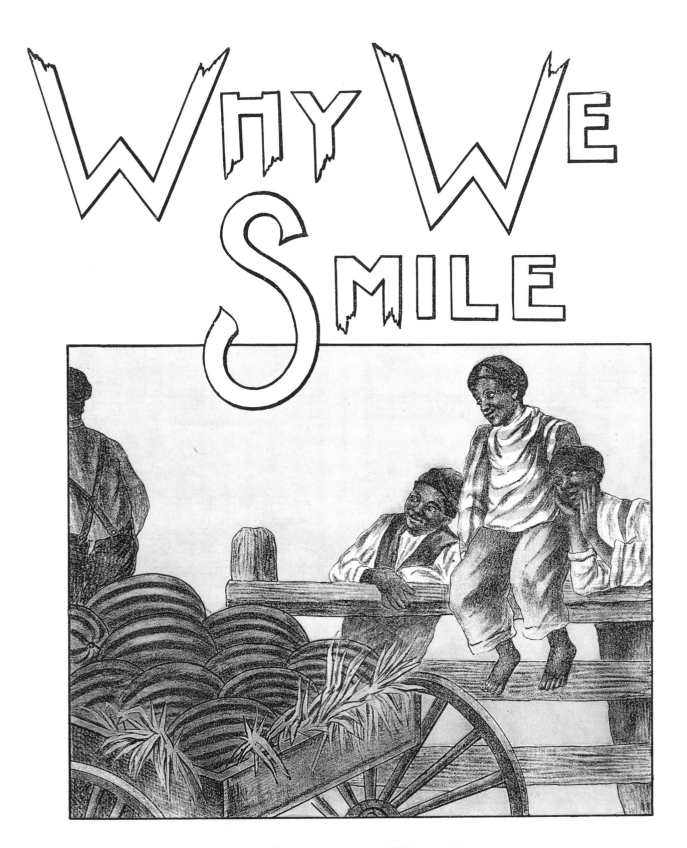

COMPOSED BY
CHAS HUNTER.
PUBLISHED BY FRANK C. FITE
NASHVILLE, TENN.

Why We Smile.

by CHARLES HUNTER.

A COON SERENADE

A COON SERENADE

BY KIND PERMISSION—J. I. AUSTEN & CO. CHICAGO.

Composed by

M. H. IRISH.

Published by

FRANK G. FITE.

NASHVILLE, TENN.

5

A Coon Serenade.

M. H. IRISH.

THE CHECKERBOARD RAG

BY
E.W. JIMERSON.

PUBLISHED BY SYNDICATE MUSIC CO. ST LOUIS, MO.

The Checkerboard.

ONE STEP.

ELIJAH W. JIMERSON.

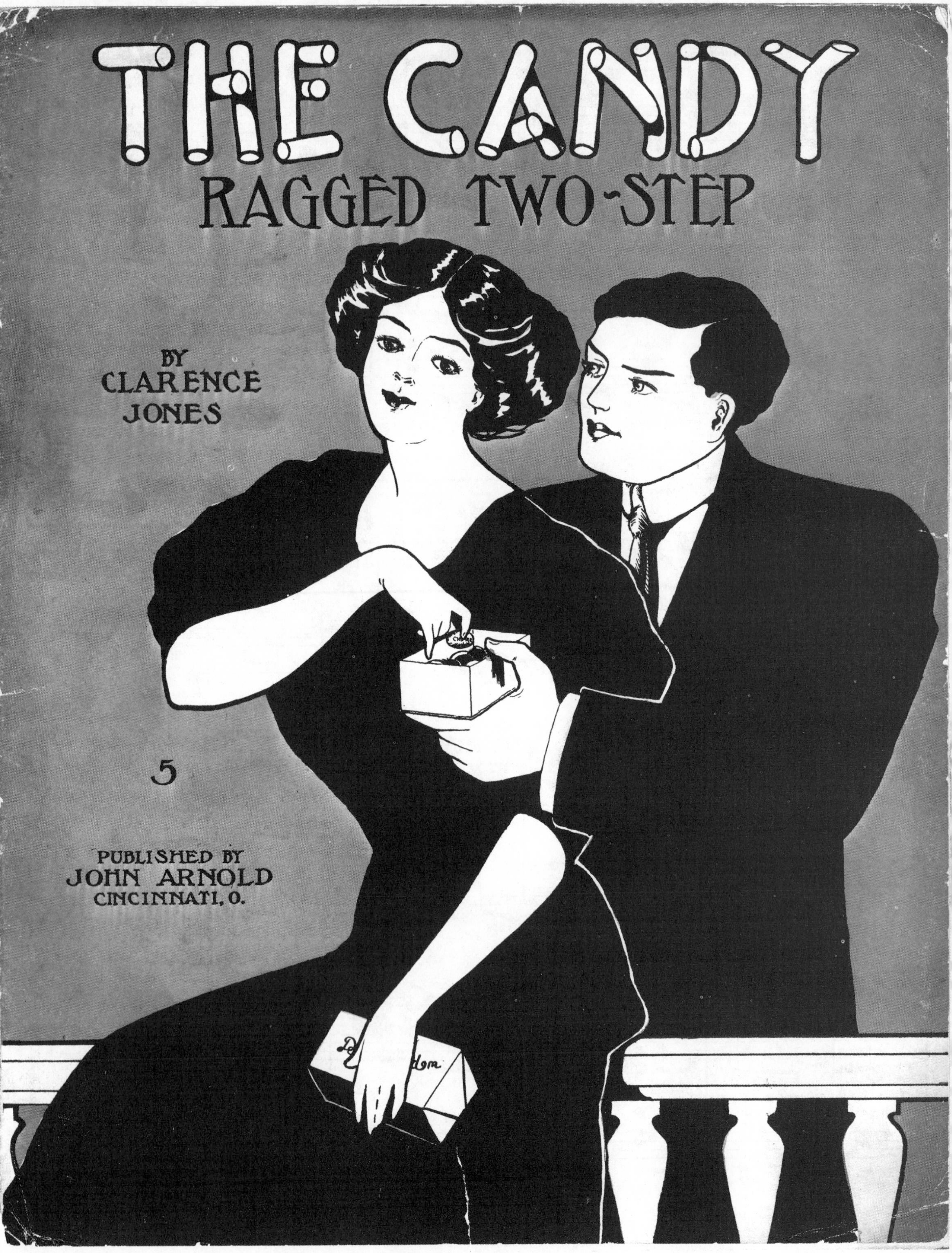
THE CANDY
RAGGED TWO-STEP
BY
CLARENCE
JONES
5
PUBLISHED BY
JOHN ARNOLD
CINCINNATI, O.

The Candy
Ragged Two Step

CLARENCE JONES
Comp. of Lightning Rag

INTRO.
Allegro moderato

146   *Clarence Jones*

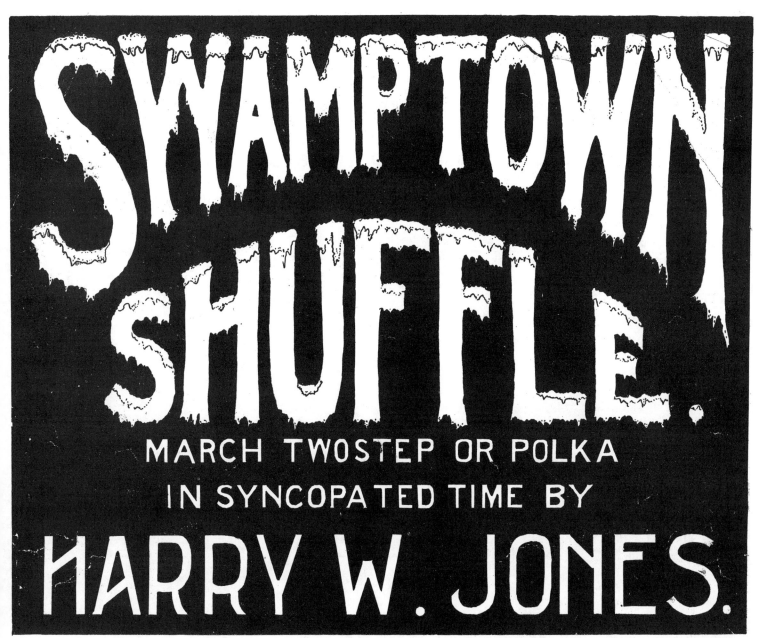

SWAMPTOWN SHUFFLE.

MARCH TWOSTEP OR POLKA
IN SYNCOPATED TIME BY

HARRY W. JONES.

Published by
MEDBERY ⑤ MUSIC CO.
(NOT INC.)
317 WASHINGTON BVD. CHICAGO ILL.

SWAMPTOWN SHUFFLE.

A SYNCOPATED TWO-STEP.

By Harry W. Jones.

TRIO.

3
J. J. J.
Rag.

JOE JORDAN.

THAT SCANDALOUS RAG

EDWIN F. KENDALL

Copyright MCMXII by The John Franklin Music Co., New York City

International Copyright Secured

Fine

B.Dr.

Trio D.C. al Fine

160   Edwin F. Kendall

DIXIE GIRL

⑤

MARCH TWO-STEP

CHARACTERISTIC

by J. BODEWALT LAMPE
COMPOSER OF "CREOLE BELLES"

WHITNEY-WARNER PUB. CO. DETROIT.

DIXIE GIRL

·CHARACTERISTIC MARCH TWO STEP·

J. BODEWALT LAMPE.

Composer of ["DREAMY EYES."
["CREOLE BELLES." etc.

OnEasyStreet

Ragtime Two-Step

By J. Reginald MacEachron

THE WHITNEY-WARNER PUBLISHING CO. DETROIT, MICH.

On Easy Street.

(IN RAGS.)

By J. REGINALD MAC EACHRON.

Author of songs
"Good Bye to all Good Bye"
"IF YOU ONLY KNEW" and Others.

Intro. Con Spirito.

I Got The Blues.

A. MAGGIO.

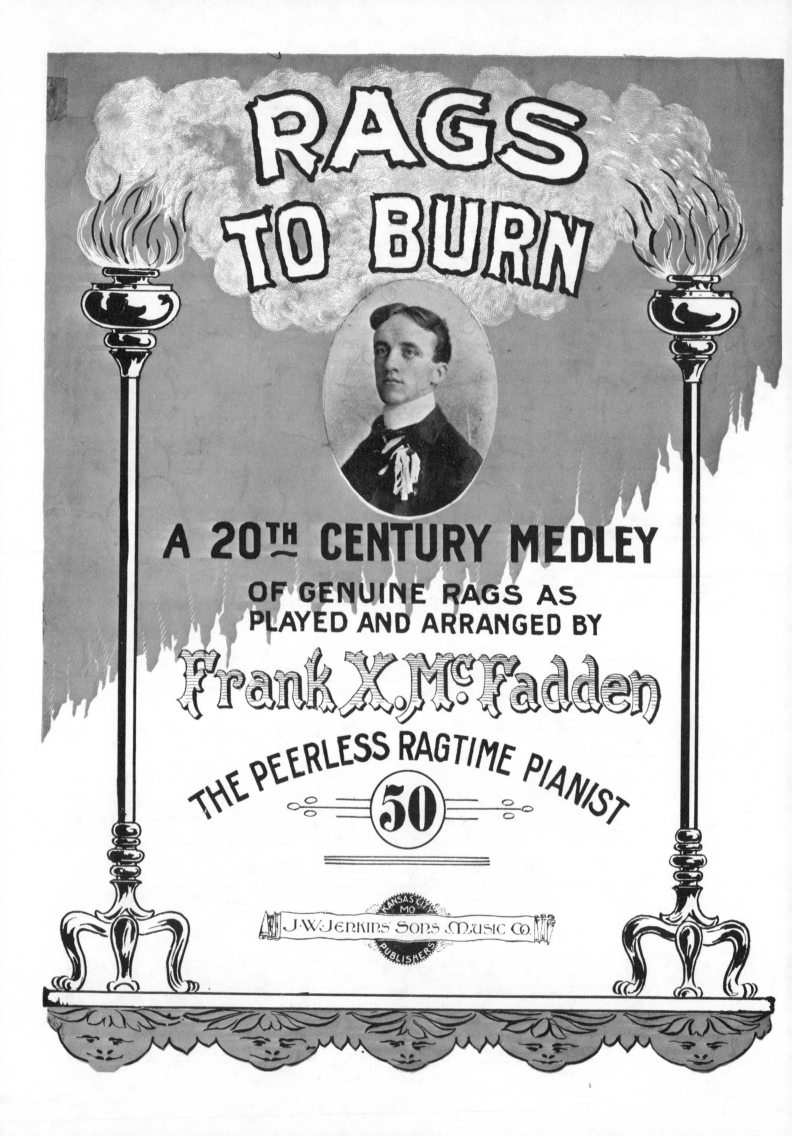

RAGS TO BURN

Frank X. Mc Fadden.

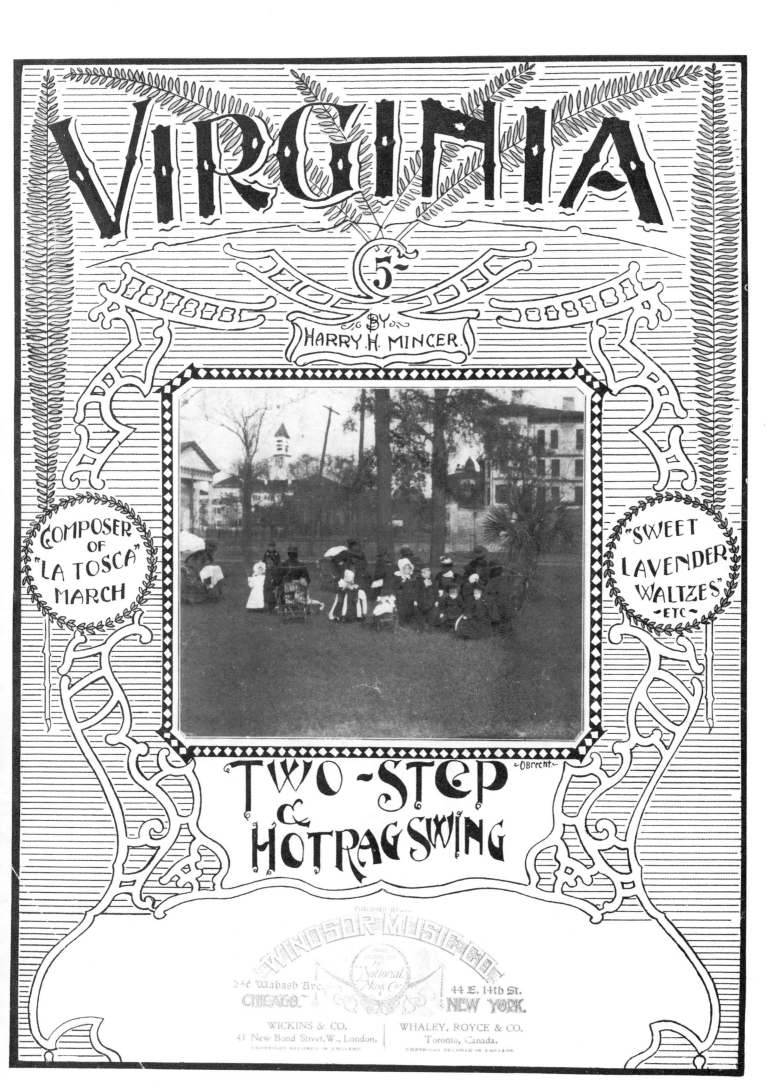

VIRGINIA TWO-STEP.

Rag-Time.

H. H. MINCER.

PIANO.

SOUR GRAPES

A RAG

BY WILL B. MORRISON

~5~

PUBLISHER
"Morrison"
147 E. MARKET ST.   INDIANAPOLIS

SOUR GRAPES

RAG

WILL B. MORRISON

Composer of
- Trouble Rag
- Scarecrow Rag
- Will o' the Wisp Waltz
- Johnnie-Jump-Ups etc. etc.

Moderato

TROUBLE
·RAG·

COMPOSED BY
MORRISON & CRABB.

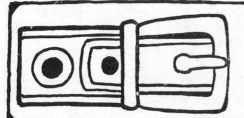

MENTEL BROS.
Publishing Company.
CINCINNATI, OHIO.

Trouble.

RAG.

MORRISON & CRABB.

Not too fast.

192   Will B. Morrison & Cecil Duanne Crabb

SCRUB RAGS

By Arthur W. Mueller.

Arnold Pub. Co.
128 W. 5th Street.
Cincinnati, Ohio.

SCRUB-RAGS.

TWO-STEP.

by ARTHUR W. MUELLER.

HORSE SHOE RAG

By

JULIA LEE NIEBERGALL

J. H. AUFDERHEIDE & CO.
MUSIC PUBLISHERS
UNITY BUILDING
INDIANAPOLIS, IND.

HORSESHOE RAG

JULIA LEE NIEBERGALL

Moderato

CANNON BALL

CHARACTERISTI
TWO STEP

BY

JOS. C. NORTHUP,

ARR. BY THOS. R. CONFARE.

Victor Kremer Company,
PUBLISHERS
Chicago, New York, London, Sydney.

"THE CANNON BALL"

CHARACTERISTIC TWO-STEP

JOS. NORTHUP

Arr. by Thos. R. Confare

LEVEE REVELS

AN AFRO-AMERICAN CANE HOP.

BY

WM. CHRISTOPHER O'HARE.

COMPOSER OF
"THE AWAKENING OF VENUS." "HELIOBAS." "COTTON PICKERS." ETC. ETC.

BAND.
ORCHESTRA.
MANDOLIN.
GUITAR.
BANJO.

PUBLISHED BY

M. WITMARK & SONS.

CHAS. SHEARD & CO. LONDON, ENG. — WHALEY ROYCE & CO. TORONTO, CAN.
COPYRIGHTED FOR GREAT BRITAIN & ALL BRITISH COLONIES & POSSESSIONS.

5

LEVEE REVELS.
AN AFRO-AMERICAN CANE-HOP.

by Wᵐ CHRISTOPHER O'HARE.

William Christopher O'Hare

FUNNY FOLKS
RAG-TIME MARCH & TWO-STEP
BY
W.C. POWELL
COMPOSER
OF
THE
GONDOLIER
6
W.C. Polla Company
PUBLISHERS
CHICAGO
U.S.A.
CHARLES. SHEARD & COMPANY
LONDON ENGLAND

FUNNY FOLKS

RAGTIME MARCH & TWO-STEP

W. C. POWELL
Comp. of "The Gondolier"

TRIO

Colonial Glide
Orchestration
25¢ NET
By
Paul Pratt.
COMPOSER OF
"WALHALLA," "VANITY RAG," ETC.
5
Rehber
MENTEL BROS. PUB. CO.
CINCINNATI, O.

Colonial Glide.

PAUL PRATT.

RAZZAZZA MAZZAZZA

AN EXTRAVAGANZA

PIANO SOLO

Arthur Pryor

⑤

PUBLISHED BY
CARL FISCHER
6-10 FOURTH AVE.
COOPER SQUARE
LONDON   NEW YORK   LEIPZIG

GASKILL MUSIC CO
212 MAIN STREET,
THE NEW WILSON-WEBB CO.
LITTLE ROCK, ARK.

"Razzazza Mazzazza"

C. Fischer's Edition.

ARTHUR PRYOR.

Piano.

The Pride of Bucktown

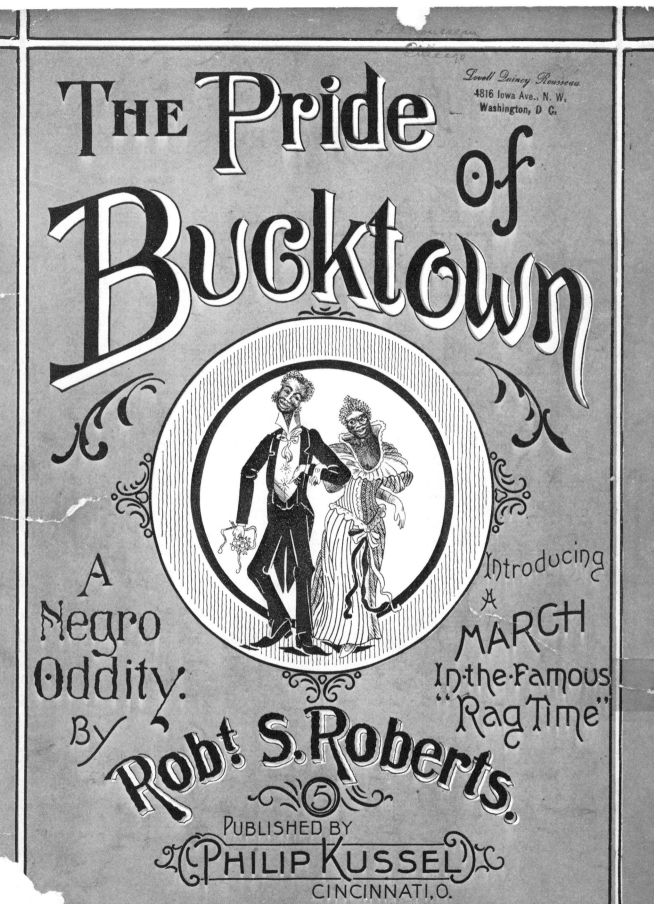

A Negro Oddity.

By Rob't S. Roberts.

Introducing A MARCH In the Famous "Rag Time"

⑤

PUBLISHED BY

PHILIP KUSSEL

CINCINNATI, O.

THE PRIDE OF BUCKTOWN.

ROBT. S. ROBERTS.

Walkin' on de Rainbow Road.
CAKE WALK and TWO STEP.

By S. M. ROBERTS.

234   S. M. Roberts

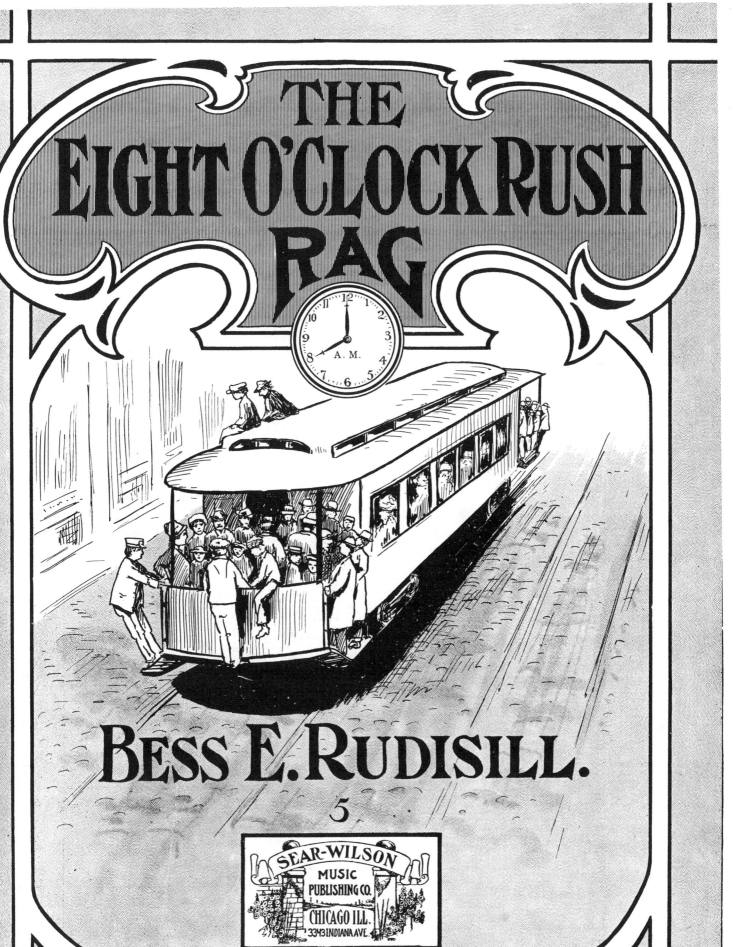

The Eight O'Clock Rush
(RAG)

BESS RUDISILL.
Arr. by Don Bestor.

Tempo di Rag.

Too Much Raspberry

FOX TROT

By SYDNEY K. RUSSELL,
Composer of
"My Flower of Waikiki," etc.

SLEEPY SIDNEY.

Rag-time Two-Step.

ARCHIE W. SCHEU.

OPHELIA RAG

BY
JAMES SCOTT
COMPOSER OF
"FROG LEGS"
GRACE & BEAUTY RAG
SUNBURST RAG

OPHELIA

DON'T CHUW THE RAG - ZING IT

OPHELIA BUMPS AND PIP GINT

PUBLISHERS OF
RAGTIME THAT IS DIFFERENT
STARK MVSIC CO
ST.LOUIS, MO.   127 EAST 23 ST
NEW YORK.

OPHELIA RAG.

JAMES SCOTT
Com. of "Frogg Legs."

Not fast.

TRIO.

PRINCESS RAG

By JAMES SCOTT

Composer of
Frog Legs Rag.
Grace & Beauty. etc.

Publishers: Stark Music Co. St Louis Mo.

THE PRINCESS RAG.

JAMES SCOTT.
Comp. of Frog Leggs Rag.

Not too fast.

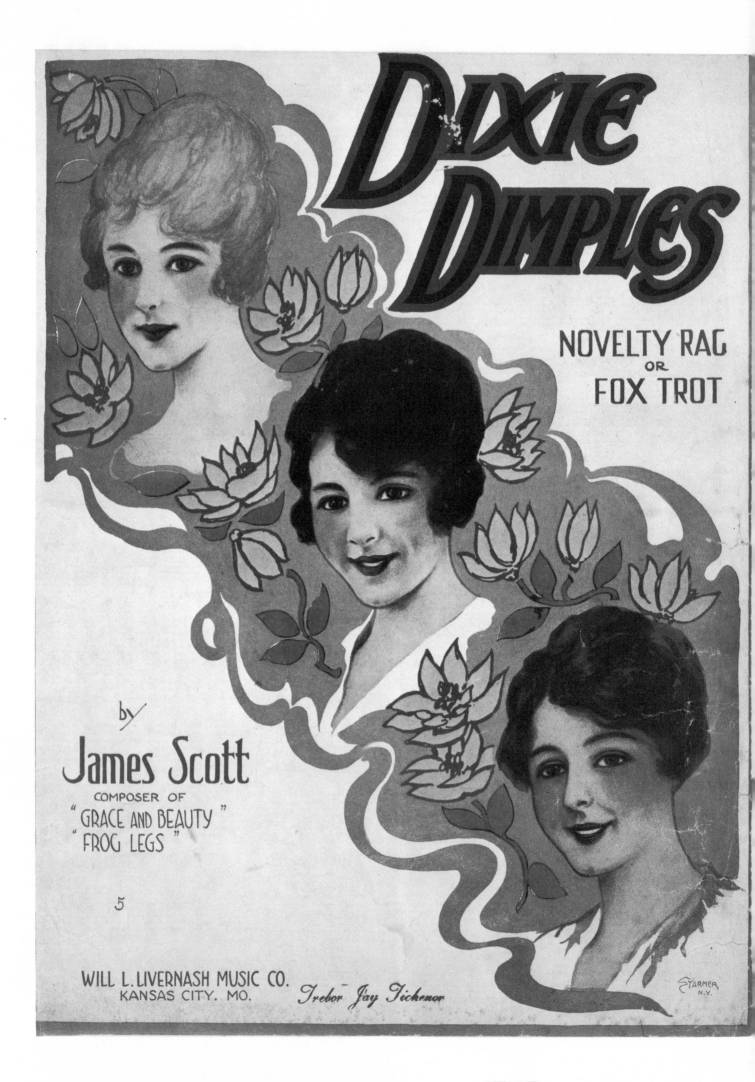

DIXIE DIMPLES
Novelty Rag Fox Trot

By JAMES SCOTT
Composer of
"GRACE AND BEAUTY RAG" etc.

258 *James Scott*

PANAMA RAG.

C. SEYMOUR.

Marcia.

Trio.

HOLY MOSES

BY· CY· SEYMOUR· 5

PUBLISHED · BY·ARNETT·DELONAIS·CO·CHICAGO

HOLY MOSES

RAG.

By C. SEYMOUR.

Con spirito.

Campin' On De Ole Suwanee.

Characteristic March.

(Two-Step, Polka, or Cake-Walk.)

Allegro moderato. *(Not too fast.)*

LEE OREAN SMITH.

PIANO.

Copyright 1899 by Vandersloot Music Co. Williamsport, Pa.

TRIO.

Trombone Johnsen

RagTime CakeWalk

PIANO 50¢
ORCHESTRA 50¢
BAND 50¢

BY

E. J. STARK

John Stark & Son
SHEET MUSIC PUBLISHERS
St. Louis, Mo.

TROMBONE JOHNSEN.

A RAGTIME CAKE WALK

By E. J. STARK.

BILLIKEN RAG
BILLIKEN
GOOD LUCK
BILLIKEN
By
E·J·Stark
5
H·REICHARD
STARK MUSIC Co.
ST. LOUIS, MO.
Trebor Jay Tichenor

Billikin Rag.

E. J. STARK.

INTRO.

Gum Shoe

FOX TROT

E. J. STARK

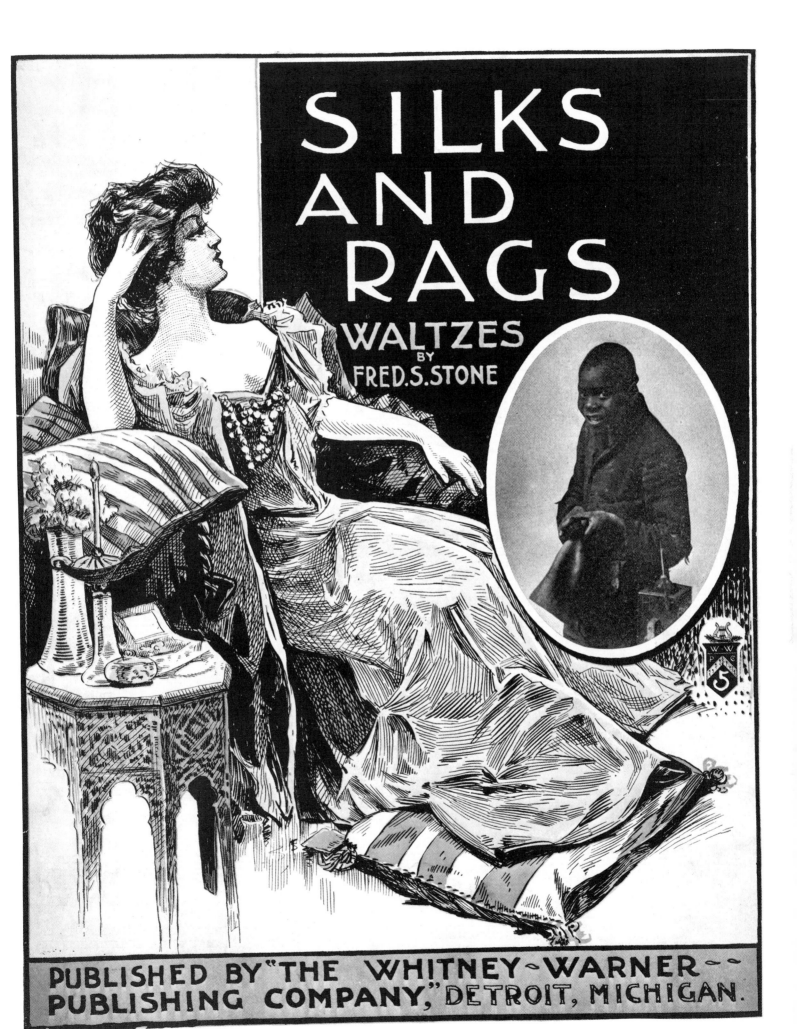

SILKS AND RAGS

WALTZES
BY
FRED. S. STONE

PUBLISHED BY "THE WHITNEY~WARNER~~ PUBLISHING COMPANY," DETROIT, MICHIGAN.

SILKS AND RAGS.
Waltzes.

FRED S. STONE.
Composer of { Ma Ragtime Baby. Lady of Quality. Elseeta etc.

a tempo

ff

D.C. al Fine.

Calla Lily Rag.

=== BY ===

LOGAN THANE,

(NAT E. SOLOMONS.)

5

PUBLISHERS OF
RAGTIME THAT IS DIFFERENT
STARK MVSIC CO.
ST. LOUIS. MO.   127 EAST 23 ST.
NEW YORK.

CALLA LILLY.
RAG.

By { LOGAN THANE.
NAT E. SOLOMONS.

Moderato marcato.

Copyright, MCMVII, by Stark Music Printing and Pub. Co.

294　*Logan Thane (Nat E. Solomons)*

296 *Logan Thane (Nat E. Solomons)*

Dover Popular Songbooks

"FOR ME AND MY GAL" AND OTHER FAVORITE SONG HITS, 1915–1917, David A. Jasen (ed.). 31 great hits: Pretty Baby, MacNamara's Band, Over There, Old Grey Mare, Beale Street, M-O-T-H-E-R, more, with original sheet music covers, complete vocal and piano. 144pp. 9 × 12.
28127-2 Pa. **$9.95**

POPULAR IRISH SONGS, Florence Leniston (ed.). 37 all-time favorites with vocal and piano arrangements: "My Wild Irish Rose," "Irish Eyes are Smiling," "Last Rose of Summer," "Danny Boy," many more. 160pp.
26755-5 Pa. **$9.95**

FAVORITE SONGS OF THE NINETIES, edited by Robert Fremont. 88 favorites: "Ta-Ra-Ra-Boom-De-Aye," "The Band Played on," "Bird in a Gilded Cage," etc. 401pp. 9 × 12.
21536-9 Pa. **$17.95**

POPULAR SONGS OF NINETEENTH-CENTURY AMERICA, edited by Richard Jackson. 64 most important songs: "Old Oaken Bucket," "Arkansas Traveler," "Yellow Rose of Texas," etc. 290pp. 9 × 12.
23270-0 Pa. **$14.95**

SONG HITS FROM THE TURN OF THE CENTURY, edited by Paul Charosh, Robert A. Fremont. 62 big hits: "Silver Heels," "My Sweetheart's the Man in the Moon," etc. 296pp. 9 × 12. (Except British Commonwealth [but may be sold in Canada])
23158-5 Pa. **$8.95**

ALEXANDER'S RAGTIME BAND AND OTHER FAVORITE SONG HITS, 1901–1911, edited by David A. Jasen. Fifty vintage popular songs America still sings, reprinted in their entirety from the original editions. Introduction. 224pp. 9 × 12. (Available in U.S. only) 25331-7 Pa. **$14.95**

"PEG O' MY HEART" AND OTHER FAVORITE SONG HITS, 1912 & 1913, edited by Stanley Appelbaum. 36 songs by Berlin, Herbert, Handy and others, with complete lyrics, full piano arrangements and original sheet music covers in black and white. 176pp. 9 × 12. 25998-6 Pa. **$12.95**

SONGS OF THE CIVIL WAR, Irwin Silber (ed.). Piano, vocal, guitar chords for 125 songs including *Battle Cry of Freedom, Marching Through Georgia, Dixie, Oh, I'm a Good Old Rebel, The Drummer Boy of Shiloh,* many more. 400pp. 8⅜ × 11.
28438-7 Pa. **$16.95**

AMERICAN BALLADS AND FOLK SONGS, John A. Lomax and Alan Lomax. Over 200 songs, music and lyrics: *Frankie and Albert, John Henry, Frog Went a-Courtin', Down in the Valley, Skip to My Lou,* other favorites. Notes on each song. 672pp. 5⅜ × 8½.
28276-7 Pa. **$13.95**

"TAKE ME OUT TO THE BALL GAME" AND OTHER FAVORITE SONG HITS, 1906–1908, edited by Lester Levy. 23 favorite songs from the turn-of-the-century with lyrics and original sheet music covers: "Cuddle Up a Little Closer, Lovey Mine," "Harrigan," "Shine on, Harvest Moon," "School Days," other hits. 128pp. 9 × 12. 24662-0 Pa. **$9.95**

THE AMERICAN SONG TREASURY: 100 Favorites, edited by Theodore Raph. Complete piano arrangements, guitar chords and lyrics for 100 best-loved tunes, "Buffalo Gals," "Oh, Suzanna," "Clementine," "Camptown Races," and much more. 416pp. 8¼ × 11. 25222-1 Pa. **$15.95**

"THE ST. LOUIS BLUES" AND OTHER SONG HITS OF 1914, edited by Sandy Marrone. Full vocal and piano for "By the Beautiful Sea," "Play a Simple Melody," "They Didn't Believe Me," 21 songs in all. 112pp. 9 × 12.
26383-5 Pa. **$9.95**

STEPHEN FOSTER SONG BOOK, Stephen Foster. 40 favorites: "Beautiful Dreamer," "Camptown Races," "Jeanie with the Light Brown Hair," "My Old Kentucky Home," etc. 224pp. 9 × 12. 23048-1 Pa. **$10.95**

ONE HUNDRED ENGLISH FOLKSONGS, edited by Cecil J. Sharp. Border ballads, folksongs, collected from all over Great Britain. "Lord Bateman," "Henry Martin," "The Green Wedding," many others. Piano. 235pp. 9 × 12.
23192-5 Pa. **$14.95**

THE CIVIL WAR SONGBOOK, edited by Richard Crawford. 37 songs: "Battle Hymn of the Republic," "Drummer Boy of Shiloh," "Dixie," 34 more. 157pp. 9 × 12.
23422-3 Pa. **$9.95**

SONGS OF WORK AND PROTEST, Edith Fowke, Joe Glazer. 100 important songs: "Union Maid," "Joe Hill," "We Shall Not Be Moved," many more. 210pp. 7⅞ × 10¼.
22899-1 Pa. **$10.95**

A RUSSIAN SONG BOOK, edited by Rose N. Rubin and Michael Stillman. 25 traditional folk songs, plus 19 popular songs by twentieth-century composers. Full piano arrangements, guitar chords. Lyrics in original Cyrillic, transliteration and English translation. With discography. 112p. 9 × 12.
26118-2 Pa. **$8.95**

FAVORITE CHRISTMAS CAROLS, selected and arranged by Charles J. F. Cofone. Title, music, first verse and refrain of 34 traditional carols in handsome calligraphy; also subsequent verses and other information in type. 79pp. 8⅛ × 11.
20445-6 Pa. **$4.95**

SEVENTY SCOTTISH SONGS, Helen Hopekirk (ed.). Complete piano and vocals for classics of Scottish song: *Flow Gently, Sweet Afton, Comin' thro' the Rye (Gin a Body Meet a Body), The Campbells are Comin', Robin Adair,* many more. 208pp. 8⅛ × 11.
27029-7 Pa. **$12.95**

35 SONG HITS BY GREAT BLACK SONGWRITERS: Bert Williams, Eubie Blake, Ernest Hogan and Others, David A. Jasen (ed.). Ballads, show tunes, other early 20th-century works by black songwriters include "Some of These Days," "A Good Man Is Hard to Find," "I'm Just Wild About Harry," "Love Will Find a Way," 31 other classics. Reprinted from rare sheet music, original covers. 160pp. 9 x 12. (USO)
40416-1 Pa. **$12.95**

"BEALE STREET" AND OTHER CLASSIC BLUES: 38 Works, 1901–1921, David A. Jasen (ed.). "St. Louis Blues," "The Hesitating Blues," "Down Home Blues," "Jelly Roll Blues," "Railroad Blues," and many more. Reproduced directly from rare sheet music (including original covers). Introduction. 160pp. 9 x 12. (USO)
40183-9 Pa. **$12.95**

"A PRETTY GIRL IS LIKE A MELODY" AND OTHER FAVORITE SONG HITS, 1918–1919, David A. Jasen (ed.). "After You've Gone," "How Ya Gonna Keep 'Em Down on the Farm," "I'm Always Chasing Rainbows," "Rock-a-Bye Your Baby" and 36 other Golden Oldies. 176pp. 9 x 12.
29421-8 Pa. **$12.95**

500 BEST-LOVED SONG LYRICS, Ronald Herder (ed.). Complete lyrics for well-known folk songs, hymns, popular and show tunes, more. "Oh Susanna," "The Battle Hymn of the Republic," "When Johnny Comes Marching Home," hundreds more. Indispensable for singalongs, parties, family get-togethers, etc. 416pp. 5⅜ x 8½.
29725-X Pa. **$10.95**

MY FIRST BOOK OF AMERICAN FOLK SONGS: 20 Favorite Pieces in Easy Piano Arrangements, Bergerac (ed.). Expert settings of traditional favorites by a well-known composer and arranger for young pianists: *Amazing Grace, Blue Tail Fly, Sweet Betsy from Pike,* many more. 48pp. 8¼ x 11.
28885-4 Pa. **$3.95**

MY FIRST BOOK OF CHRISTMAS SONGS: 20 Favorite Songs in Easy Piano Arrangements, Bergerac (ed.). Beginners will love playing these beloved favorites in easy arrangements: "Jingle Bells," "Deck the Halls," "Joy to the World," "Silent Night," "Away in a Manger," "Hark! The Herald Angels Sing," 14 more. Illustrations. 48pp. 8¼ x 11.
29718-7 Pa. **$3.95**